GO!

Go Deep | Go Wide | Go Together

You Can Read the Bible With Confidence!

GO!

GO DEEP | GO WIDE | GO TOGETHER

SUSTAINABLE STRATEGIES FOR
ENGAGING GOD'S WORD

PAM GILLASPIE

GO! SUSTAINABLE STRATEGIES FOR
ENGAGING GOD'S WORD

Copyright ©2024, 2026 by Pam Gillaspie

ISBN 978-1-960938-21-3

Design: Dave Gillaspie

Revised printing 2026
Printed in the United States of America.

Table of Contents

With love for my family.
Follow Him with your whole hearts!

*For the eyes of the Lord move to and fro throughout the earth
that He may strongly support those whose heart
is completely His.*

II Chronicles 16:9a

Acknowledgments

Thank you to my family for bearing through this process with me and allowing me to tell some of our family stories to help others along on the journey. My love for you is deeper than words. Thank you, Dave, for encouraging the rewrite and for your beautiful layout and cover design. Mom and Dad, you did the hard, day-in-and-day-out work of Deuteronomy 6 that set me on a path to knowing God—I am forever grateful to you. Cress VanderMeersch, there are no better eyes in the business! Thank you for your editorial and proofreading work on this project and for being my primary Hebrews listener back in the day. (Readers, any typos you may find are almost certainly misses that I made on corrections that Cress caught!) Thank you to my ministry partner team who previewed the material, kept me on track through the rewriting process, and offered encouragement that propelled me forward on days I was ready to quit. Thank you to Mary Ann for being the glue that holds so many things together, and to Olivia for bringing fresh ideas to the table. Finally, all glory to God who prepares good works in advance that we should walk in them.

Introduction

THIRTY YEARS INTO MINISTRY and I still don't know it all—no one does—but I've learned much along the way. In my early 30s I wrote my first book called *No More Excuses: An Almost Too Practical Guide to Reading through the Bible*. As I approached 40, it was re-released by a new publisher with updated material as *Ablaze: Igniting Spiritual Passion for Life through Reading God's Word*.

Shortly after the release of *Ablaze*, I began writing inductive Bible studies for Precept Ministries which consumed most of my time and energy for the next 15 or so years of my life.

No More Excuses and *Ablaze* focused primarily on reading God's Word widely by giving practical helps to people who wanted to read through the whole Bible. My time writing inductive Bible studies focused primarily on helping people study God's Word deeply. The two-fold approach of reading widely and studying deeply has been at the core of my Bible reading/study philosophy since college.

For several years now, my husband has been encouraging me to give the *Ablaze* title a refresh since many of the practical helps that I offered in the original book are now out of date in our digital and web-connected world. As someone who always wants to push the ball forward, the idea of rewriting an already published work is near anathema to me. Still, as times changes we must necessarily adapt and retool where needed.

If you have read *Ablaze,* you will find in this current edition much of the material that I addressed in that book, material that has stood the test of time and remains unaffected by the technological changes in our world over the past twenty years. I hope you will also find an increased depth of encouragement and insight from someone who is now closer to the end of their ministry life than the beginning, lessons from walking in the Word, with the Lord, and with His people on a longer trail than the author of my previous book had!

As I've mentioned, my philosophy of spiritual growth in God's Word has long been that of reading widely and studying deeply. I've had words to describe that since I was 18 years old. People who know me know that I am all about **deep** and **wide** in the Word! The additional piece that I have lived for nearly my whole life but have not adequately put into words is this: **together.** When we go deep and wide in the Word and when we do this in community—when we do it together—we have a recipe for sustained spiritual growth and reproducible impact.

Go deep, go wide, and go together provides a basic structure for individuals or small groups of believers looking to grow through engagement in God's Word. Because it is a general pattern for growth, it can also come alongside and integrate with existing church and parachurch ministries, particularly helping to fill in gaps that sometimes develop in single-minded organizations.

All this to say, this book is not a manifesto to follow me or a particular system. It is a call to follow Jesus fully through His Word and by His Spirit. It is an encouragement to the church universal to follow Jesus together!

So use the principles you find here with your Precept group, your Bible Study Fellowship people, your AWANA kids, or your adult Bible study. Use it to strengthen your campus ministry, your prison ministry, or wherever God has called you together with other believers. Use the principles if you're Protestant, use them if you're Catholic, use them if you're Orthodox.

Let's go deep and wide in the Word and grow up together to maturity and in unity! This is but one simple guide to biblical literacy and spiritual growth. There are many. I pray that this one helps some.

Pam Gillaspie
2024

CHAPTER 1

A Question That Changed My Life

"So you've read through the whole Bible, right?"

WHEN I FIRST READ THROUGH THE BIBLE in the 1990s, I faced the challenge of reading an 80-hour book with difficult sections—just like people do today—but the only technological distractions in my world were ABC, NBC, and CBS.

As our world has changed and accelerated in pace, the thought of reading the Bible regularly, much less reading the whole thing, can seem overwhelming, particularly considering the digital onslaught each of us faces every single day.

Even though my '90s world was simpler, I understand the overwhelm. I understand the failure of having tried and fallen short. I understand the angst. I first read through the Bible in my mid-20s which, I suppose, is earlier than most, but I had my share of failed attempts, false starts, and doubts along the way even in a decidedly non-digital world. Digital technology can boost us into the Word in new and exciting ways, but the corresponding challenges of technology are daunting.

While the Bible is more accessible to more people in more forms than ever before in history, Bible engagement continues to drop. According to 2023 research from the American Bible Society, "Fewer people in America are engaging with the Bible. Scripture engagement is not rising yet; it continues on a downward trajectory."[1] While statistics and data are notoriously slippery, a scan of the cultural climate provides a good sanity check. A quick look around shows cultural behavior increasingly deviates from biblical truth.

Add to that the fact that we read less. Our attention spans are declining, and our intake of media in various forms boxes out not only the Bible, but literary classics and other books as well.

READING IS DOWN

Bible reading aside, people today read fewer books. While I'm tempted to dive down this rabbit hole, let me leave you with just a couple statistics from 2022: over 50% of American adults reported reading either no books or only one book the prior year. When including audio books, 33% of American adults "read" between zero and one book a year.[2] Certainly many read more, but the societal trends away from reading books are staggering. (Give yourself a sticker for being an outlier!)

> *Bible reading aside, people today read fewer books.*

DISTRACTIONS ARE UP

While books are trending down, we all know what is trending up: social media. Statista, a global data and business intelligence platform, reports

---

1. American Bible Society. State of the Bible, USA 2023. https://1s712.americanbible.org/state-of-the-bible/stateofthebible/State_of_the_bible-2023.pdf

2. You.Gov. What kinds of books did Americans read growing up, and what do they read now? https://today.yougov.com/entertainment/articles/43285-books-americans-read-growing-up-and-now?redirect_from=%2Ftopics%2Fentertainment%2Farticles-reports%2F2022%2F07%2F29%2Fbooks-americans-read-growing-up-and-now

that in 2023 internet users spent 151 minutes each day on social media.[3] It doesn't take a scholar or researcher to connect the dots here. Almost everyone knows firsthand the impact technology has had on how we think, concentrate, and live.

I am grateful that I was able to read through the Bible the first time without the additional challenges that the digital age poses, but I have still found myself having to adapt and change. Technology distractions come crashing into all of our lives—but there is hope!

MY STORY IN THE WORD

As I've said, I first read through the Bible in my 20s already having a history of Bible-reading failure under my belt. That was strange for me as I didn't see failure as an option for anything in my 20s.

I've mellowed over the years, but in my 20s I did what I set out to do. Always. Double major? Sure! Twenty-two credit hours in a semester just for fun? Why not? Greek? Bring it! Greek exegesis with grad students? We're this far, let's go!

You've probably guessed the one word I'd use to describe my 20-something self: DRIVEN. We could certainly add competitive and probably arrogant to the list, too; I'm sure my family would.

GENESIS IN JANUARY

When I set out to read through the Bible for myself January after January and proceeded to fail January after January, you can imagine my frustration (not to mention my feelings of failure). Perhaps you've ridden the Genesis-in-January train. The January resolve gives you that burst of hope, the "attaboys" from those you tell that you're "going to read through the Bible this year" spur you on. It's not unlike the confidence boost people experience as they tell their friends that they're "pre-med"— that is, until they run into organic chemistry. As organic chemistry is to pre-med students, so is Leviticus to would-be through-the-Bible readers.

---

3. Statista. Daily time spent on social networking by internet users worldwide from 2012 to 2024. https://www.statista.com/statistics/433871/daily-social-media-usage-worldwide/

The end of December offers such hope with an entire year to cross the finish line and yet most people fall off the train once the journey starts into the laws and building plans at the end of Exodus. That's about twenty-two days in on a basic Bible reading plan that starts with Genesis 1 on January 1.

THE STEEP HILL OF LEVITICUS AND NUMBERS

Leviticus wipes out most of those who survive the latter chapters of Exodus. Some people make it through organic chemistry, which is why we have doctors today, and some people make it through Leviticus, but most people don't. Most don't even survive Exodus.

> *Some people make it through organic chemistry, which is why we have doctors today and some people make it through Leviticus, but most people don't. Most don't even survive Exodus.*

That was, more or less, my experience year after year starting in my late teens. Every year I'd start in the 50-chapter book of Genesis—the Bible does not open with a short on-ramp. I don't remember the exact details, just the overwhelming sense of dropping off in the Torah each and every year.

You likely know exactly what I mean. Most people have experienced the frustration of finally making it through Genesis (50 chapters) only to face an uphill climb with the introduction of the Law of Moses and the step-by-step instructions for building a tabernacle at the end of Exodus (40 chapters) followed immediately by an even steeper climb with the detailed laws of Leviticus (27 chapters). Make it through those and you end up staring at all of the numbers in the beginning of Numbers (36 chapters) before circling back around to a recapping of the Mosiac Law in Deuteronomy (34 chapters). If you have any nerd in you, you can probably "hear" the content in the name of Deuteronomy—*deutero* (second) and *nomos* (law), at which time you might be thinking, "Wasn't once enough with the Law?"

GIVING UP . . . AGAIN

The fact that my normal grit and tenacity failed to carry me into the historical books frustrated and discouraged me to the point that I eventually gave up, deciding that reading through the Bible would be something that I would eventually do when I was older. It astonishes me how effective repeated failure can be at discouraging us and causing learned helplessness. You may be sitting here right now thinking, "I've never been able to do this before, why will this time be any different?" Some people discount themselves without ever trying, assuming failure from the start; others try and fail repeatedly. With each failure, it is harder to start again. If that is you, listen carefully: there is hope!

> *With each failure, it is harder to start again. If that is you, listen carefully: there is hope!*

I'm so grateful that God, in His mercy, intervened in my mire of discouragement and learned helplessness. It was not long after I had officially given up during my 20s that God would call me not only *to* His Word, but also *through* His Word. This process of reading the Bible widely became formative in my spiritual development.

A SIDE ROAD ALONG THE WAY

During this season of what I would have termed Bible-reading failure, God began building my spiritual foundation in another way, an ancient way quite counter to how we typically approach learning today. I began to memorize Scripture. Memorizing had been a way of life for me throughout my childhood, particularly starting in the fifth grade when our church began participating in the AWANA youth program. Taken from 2 Timothy 2:15, AWANA stands for Approved Workmen Are Not Ashamed. Children and teens are discipled primarily through athletics and Bible memorization, two of my core competencies. (Did I mention that I'm competitive?) In a world where every child did not get a trophy simply for showing up, the trophy earned for the Timothy Award (equaling about 300 verses memorized) called to me. I memorized for trophies

7

as a child—base motives for sure, but the Word of God does not return void.

I dove back into memorizing as a young 20-something after several try-and-fail attempts at Bible reading. My clinician friends reading this have likely already diagnosed my lean toward the cognitive distortion of all-or-nothing thinking, but in one of my biggest all-or-nothing decisions, God met me and changed my life. The year was 1990 and our new pastor, the Rev. Joe Boerman, announced that he would be preaching from the book of Hebrews for the next . . . year. "Hebrews?" I thought, "For a year? Are you kidding me?" He was not.

ALL OR NOTHING

When he first arrived at Immanuel Church, then in Waukegan, Illinois, Pastor Joe taught through the Gospel of John on Sunday mornings and the book of Joshua on Sunday nights, back when church was still a split-double-header event. After several years of interim pastors and general unease in the pews, we finally had a shepherd who would tend the flock for the next 25 years. Our church had a sense of proper stability again, but those words about Hebrews nearly had me packing. My general reaction to the epistle to the Hebrews came from fear. The specific fear came from Hebrews 6 and 10.

While I hadn't read through the Bible at this point in my life, I had read through the New Testament and knew that Hebrews had a couple of difficult passages that sounded on the surface like it may be possible for a person to lose their salvation. I wanted nothing to do with Hebrews. I wanted John 3:16 (God so loved the world), John 10:27-29 (no one can pluck me out of the Father's hand), and Ephesians 2:8-9 (salvation is a gift).

I had loved the John series and Joshua, but Hebrews?! My all-or-nothing thinking led me to two possible options:
1. Fold. Leave the church for a year and worship elsewhere.
2. Go all in. Memorize the book of Hebrews as Pastor Joe preached through it.

I choose option two. It changed my life.

LEANING INTO THE HARD QUESTIONS

I had made a similar decision several years earlier as a sophomore in college, a decision to lean into rather than pull away from a difficult text that had been a pebble in my shoe since the fifth grade. There are moments in life that we never forget, events frozen in time that we can recall with clarity. I think of the planes crashing into the World Trade Center, the report during my college chapel that the space shuttle Columbia had exploded, and the first time I read the full book of Romans, specifically the first time I read Romans 9 (thanks to an AWANA assignment) and the chilling words attributed to God Himself, "Jacob have I loved, but Esau have I hated" (KJV). I was lying on the red shag carpet of our family room floor reading my red King James Bible inscribed with my name on the cover when those words—can I say this?—assaulted me.

For years I looked away, averting my eyes from that God I hadn't met in Sunday School, from that God who the text told me hated Esau.

> For years I looked away, averting my eyes from that God I hadn't met in Sunday School, from that God who the text told me hated Esau.

As a sophomore at Wheaton College, I faced my Romans 9 fears head on during my class on that New Testament epistle and chose Romans 9 as the topic of my term paper. Yes, I earned my A, but more importantly, I made a step toward taking my questions to God instead of stuffing them down and ignoring them. My new approach stemmed from a Wheaton class my freshman year with Dr. Vic Gordon who encouraged us to ask questions, because the God of the Bible can stand up to anything we can bring. To think that my 18-year-old brain could conjure up the one question that would undo God was ludicrous. Up to that point, though, I honestly thought it could! Maybe you can relate.

FROM ROMANS 9 TO HEBREWS

Four years after diving headlong into Romans 9, I made the decision to baptize myself in the epistle to the Hebrews. The early weeks of memorizing proved relatively easy. Having taken Greek at Wheaton, my memorizing muscles remained toned and the external pacing that came from following the preaching schedule gave me the structure I needed. I'll get into more of the specifics of memorizing both verses and larger portions of Scripture later in the book, but for now let it suffice that immersing myself for a year in one book of the Bible, and a theologically and Christologically dense book at that, grew me in ways that were beyond what I could have anticipated or even hoped.

In memorizing Hebrews, God grew me in discipline of heart and mind as the only way to memorize that volume of content is literally to meditate on it night and day as the psalmist talks about in Psalm 119. It gave me confidence in the Word of God because as I wrestled with the difficult passages, I did so in fully considered context. This New Testament letter so rich in Old Testament thought and fulfillment also began cultivating a deeper appreciation in me for the Old Testament as it tied to New Testament fulfillment. When I made the crazy all-or-nothing decision and decided to push the chips to the center of the table, I had no idea how this decision to throw myself on God would turn out. I had no lofty plans for spiritual growth that I recall. I just decided to bet on the fact that pressing into the hard stuff of Scripture instead of

> *I was betting on God to show up and meet me in my doubt and fear . . . and He did. It's what He does.*

retreating would pay off. I was betting on God to show up and meet me in my doubt and fear . . . and He did. It's what He does.

MY ACCIDENTAL DEGREE

I majored in Biblical Studies at Wheaton College entirely by accident. My plan was always journalism as far back as I can remember. My plan was the Medill School of Journalism at Northwestern University, my dad's alma mater and a school not too far away. My parents' plans differed. "The Investors" wanted their only daughter and the associated tuition dollars to go to a Christian institution of higher learning. The only school that remotely interested me was Wheaton, and so I went grudgingly with the understanding that I could put in my two years and then transfer to a proper school of journalism.

As it turned out, the Bible and Theology classes that I took "since I was there" surprised me. I enjoyed them to the extent that I eventually decided to stay at Wheaton and double major in Communications (as close to journalism as it got in the western suburbs of Chicago) and Biblical Studies. I was still focused on journalism, either print or broadcast; the Bible was just interesting, nothing to put on a resume or think of as a career path. It wasn't until years later that I'd realized the core of journalism—getting at the who, what, when, where, why, and how of things—is also the heart of inductive Bible study, another critical piece in my spiritual foundation.

FALLING INTO GREEK

While I'm aware that my 16 hours of Greek at Wheaton look pretty heady on the surface, the reason I picked Greek is because I can't speak French. Turns out memorizing French vocabulary during my algebra class in high school was a poor long-term strategy. Most liberal arts colleges require some type of foreign language proficiency for graduation. At Wheaton that meant 12 credit hours. If you'd taken foreign language in high school like they tell you to do, they expected you to jump into a more advanced class where you'd actually have to speak the stuff. I hadn't taken French since my sophomore year of high school. I had scored an A every semester only because my smart friends took German and the French teacher graded on a curve. My quick short-term memory got me through Warren Township High School, but there was not a chance of that happening at Wheaton.

The one thing that I learned about foreign languages in high school is that I don't have an ear for them. I'm okay if I'm reading and writing, but hearing and speaking . . . well, not so *tres bien*. Turns out you don't have to actually speak dead languages, and that is why this girl ended up with 16 hours of Greek. It's as though God in His sovereignty knew what was coming! Go figure! Over thirty years removed from Wheaton, it is a rare day when I don't interact with Greek in one way or another. Who'd have thought?!

The undergraduate degree in Biblical Studies equipped me for lifelong study of the Bible. As any honest and semi-observant undergrad will tell you, what struck me most about my knowledge upon leaving college was the overwhelming realization of what I did not know. And yet, I had a foundation and I had tools. I'd read through much of the Bible in college—all of the New Testament to be sure—but not the whole thing. That day, though, was on a nearer horizon than I imagined.

LEARNING TO STUDY

My love of deep Bible study began when I was a sophomore in college, specifically during my class on the book of Romans. There I met lifelong friends in Strong's Concordance, Bauer's Lexicon, Moulton and Milligan's Englishman's Greek Concordance, Kittel's 10-Volume New Testament Dictionary of the Greek New Testament, and more. Dr. Alan Johnson's excitement for the text of Scripture spilled out on me. I learned the skills of reading a text through in one sitting and in several translations, of asking questions of the text, of engaging rather than disengaging from difficult passages. I learned how to think of the whole argument of a text rather than picking and choosing segments. I learned once and for all the meaning of the Greek word *logizomai*. (It means "to credit to one's account"—I got it wrong on a test, but that's another story for another day!) In short, Bible study hooked me. I had no vocational thoughts attached to it; I enjoyed the study and it engaged my brain if not always my heart and soul.

THE EARLY BIBLE STUDY DAYS

Because of this academic background in biblical studies, as you might imagine I became a bit of a Bible study snob and had no desire to hang out with women and all of the feelings in what I thought constituted "Women's Bible Studies." In my zeal to parse Greek verbs I overlooked the fact that Jesus called (and calls) common people from all different walks of life to be on mission and in deep fellowship with Him. Good thing, because I, too, am just a common person, but at 22 the intellectual pride was real. I take solace in the fact that I'm probably not alone in this.

While still in my early 20s, I was introduced to *Precept Upon Precept* Bible studies by my pastor's wife, Debbie Boerman. These studies, based on the inductive study method of observing, interpreting, and applying Scripture gave me both the freedom and the structure to study like I had in college, and to meaningfully exegete the text. Exegesis simply means to draw out the meaning of Scripture.

Memorizing and deep study were the first two anchors in my adult life with regard to my spiritual growth. The encouragement I needed to read through the Bible took a little longer to land. But like other significant events along the way, I can point back to a moment of life change, to the specific place and time.

A QUESTION THAT CHANGED MY LIFE

It was a Tuesday morning in the early 1990s at a McDonald's on Sheridan Road in Zion, Illinois, a small city just south of Wisconsin's cheddar curtain, just west of Lake Michigan when a high school junior asked me a question that would alter the course of my life: "You've read through the whole Bible, right?"

"You've read through the whole Bible, right?"

Ever been asked that one yourself? It was the first time for me and I did not have a straight answer to offer back. Alicia and I had been meeting on Tuesday mornings as part of a discipleship program. She had made a decision to follow Jesus at a youth retreat and I was helping to get her established in her new faith. Each week, over an Egg McMuffin, we'd go over the basics of the Christian faith—God the Father, God the Son, God the Holy Spirit, and other core Christian concepts.

13

When we dove into the topic of Scripture, the Word of God, she dropped her question on me assuming I'd answer, "Of course, I have!" Remember, I was the 20-something adult in the situation telling this kid that she should bank her here-and-now and her forever-after on the words in this book, which as she would soon find out, I had not taken the time to fully read and investigate for myself.

My stammering answer of "I've read through the whole New Testament several times and most of the Old Testament in college" seemed to satisfy her, but the weight of my own duplicity crushed me. I heard the problem in my answer even if she hadn't. I told her that the Bible was the very Word of God and yet I hadn't made time to read it all for myself. As you already know, I had tried. Genuinely. But I had also failed and punted. I knew enough verses and facts to get by. In fact, without a direct question I doubt anyone would have guessed that I hadn't read the whole Bible. I knew, but without that direct query I likely would have continued on for who knows how long before trying again at reading the full counsel of God, because failure takes a toll.

> *I heard the problem in my answer even if she hadn't. I told her that the Bible was the very Word of God and yet I hadn't made time to read it all for myself.*

FACING MY OWN WEAKNESS

So what changed? When faced head-on with the question, I finally realized my inability to follow God on my own. For me to follow, I need Him to power my obedience. We all do! Whether you're a new follower of Jesus or a lifelong pastor, whether you're a reader or a listener, whether you love to study or not . . . every single one of us needs the Holy Spirit to grow and live the Christians life.

Because I was raised in a Christian home, I never thought I could work my way to God. I *did* think I was getting in on the coattails of the family name for awhile (my grandpa was the pastor when I was little!), but work-your-way-to-God was never something that I thought anyone could do. Turns out, though, I struggled with a variation of it. In my pride my life betrayed an implicit belief that Jesus saves and Pam sanctifies. I can't work my way to God, but by golly, I better behave on my own once He has saved me. The lie is subtle, as the most powerful ones always are.

You may be believing the same lie. The lie says, "Jesus saved you and now you better muscle up and get on living like a Christian by your own grit and tenacity." It was through failure, check that, it was through *repeated* failure that I came to realize my grit can't power the sanctification train. That's a job for the Holy Spirit.

> *It was through failure, check that, it was through repeated failure that I came to realize my grit can't power the sanctification train. That's a job for the Holy Spirit.*

ASKING FOR HELP

I can put words to it now, but in the moment all I could do was to cry out to God for help. "Lord, I know that it is Your will that I read Your Word (I did know enough truth to know this!) and I know that if I ask something according to Your will that You will hear me and answer it (that was from 1 John 5). I believe it is Your will that I know all of Your Word, but clearly I cannot do it on my own. Would You give me a desire for Your Word? Would You help me to know when I can read and where I should read? Would You help me know what I need to get rid of to make the time in my schedule to read?"

I finally stopped trying to follow Jesus by my own power and threw myself on His power to not only save me, but to sanctify me (for more on this, see Galatians 2 and 3).

I did not see a light shine down from heaven. I heard no audible voice. I just went about my life behaving as though He heard me and would answer. I think the first answer came in my decision not to start my reading in Genesis. Come on, if you've tried and failed a couple of times to read through beginning in January, you're probably a Genesis pro, too. I'd already read Genesis several times and I knew that Exodus and Leviticus had both bucked me off the horse before. I decided to start in the engaging and narrative-heavy book of 1 Samuel.

I started paying attention to the empty spaces in my life when I could easily work in time to read, and before long I realized clearly what needed to go. I didn't have to purge any great sin in my life to make time to read, but I noticed that I spent an undue amount of time reading both the sports section of the *Chicago Sun Times* and *Sports Illustrated* (still a weekly magazine at the time) from cover to cover. Those were my critical time drains. I cancelled both and slotted the Bible into any spare time that I had. I knew that God was answering my prayer as He guided me through simple changes and began creating a true desire for His Word in me. I started learning to go both deep and wide in God's Word.

DEEP AND WIDE IN THE WORD

It was Dr. Vic Gordon (the same Dr. Gordon who challenged his freshmen students to ask questions), then chaplain of Wheaton College and my Theology of Culture professor, who challenged our class to make a life priority of reading widely and studying deeply. Don't be just a mile deep in one subject, neither be merely a mile wide knowing very little about very much. Rather make a life practice to go both deep and wide in pursuit of knowledge.

> *Read widely, know the whole counsel of God's Word and how it fits together; study deeply to know intimately what the text means and how it applies in life.*

I'm not sure how much my dad spent on my college education, but those words were gold! They have framed my entire approach to learning, particularly to learning the Bible. Read widely, know the whole counsel of God's Word and how it fits together; study deeply to know intimately what the text means and how it applies in life.

Studying deeply came much more easily to me than reading widely as I think it does with many who have a bent towards academics, but it has been in wide reading that I've found joy and wonder far beyond expectation.

Bible memorization, deep study, and wide reading anchored my spiritual growth and we'll spend time looking at each area individually during our time together. We'll also look at one other key component that cuts against the American ethos. As I look back on my life, this interplayed with every other area more than I even realized at the time. Some would call it community, others fellowship. I like to term it the *one-anothering* of the Christian life, or *going together*. I'll tell you more about this as we go along . . . together!

GO DEEP · GO WIDE · GO TOGETHER

DRAW NEAR THIS WEEK

As you go along throughout your week, pick one—or more—of the opportunities for drawing near. Some days you'll have more time than usual. Other days you'll be so busy and stressed that you'll find drawing near to God to be your only refuge. Some days you'll have runny noses running around the house or other fires to put out, and you may not be able to draw near to God through His Word as much as you'd like.

Would you do something for me? Would you resolve right now that this will be okay? Decide that you won't go overboard and take the attitude, "If I can't do as much as I think I should, I'm not going to do anything at all." Let's decide today that some is better than none.

So, now's your chance. Ask God to guide you by His Spirit and let's begin learning to draw near to Him by reading and considering one or more of the following:

- Read John 15–17 and focus on Jesus' high priestly prayer in chapter 17. Commit to memory one or several key verses on prayer.
- Read some or all of John's Gospel account.
- Read the Sermon on the Mount located in Matthew 5–7 to see what else Jesus has to say about making requests of the Father.

DISCUSS TOGETHER

These questions can be used in a discussion group if you're using this book in a Bible study setting or book club. You can also use them to process through what you're learning on your own.

- What challenges have you faced in reading the Bible?
- What is your favorite book of the Bible and why?
- What have you found to be the most difficult book of the Bible that you've read and why?
- What do you find more difficult, reading widely or studying deeply? Why?
- What, if any, has been your best deep Bible study experience?
- Have you ever read through the Bible?
  - If so, how did you go about it?
  - If you've tried and failed, what tripped you up?
- Have you ever memorized Scripture? What was your experience?
- Do you have others who encourage you and discuss what you're reading with you?
  - If so, how has that gone?
  - If not, would you be open to praying for this?
- What do you hope will be different in your life after reading this book?
- Why do you read—or want to read—the Bible? Why do you think that reading the Bible is important?
- Where have you been reading in the Word this week? What have you been learning? What questions are you asking?

READ TOGETHER

If you're meeting with a group, spend some of your time reading the Bible aloud. Take turns with each person reading a chapter. If you have a larger group, break up into smaller groups of no more than five people each. If anyone in the group does not want to read aloud, they can simply follow along while others read. There's always someone in the group who'd love a second turn!

Read **1 John** as a group this week. It should take you less than 20 minutes. As you read, note how John describes the characteristics of people who know Jesus.

When you are finished, pray for one another; pray that you will have the desire to know God through His Word and that He will guide you with the specifics of how you can overcome any barriers that currently stand in your way.

CHAPTER 2

Finding Your Why

Why do *you* want to read the Bible?

WITH READING HABITS trending south and the Bible taking anywhere from 60 to 80 hours to read, it doesn't take a statistical analyst to see a problem. A culture rapidly losing its engagement in books will see biblical literacy vanish without clear hope of rebound on the horizon. You, though, are already a statistical outlier because you're reading this book. Unless you've picked this up with the intent of being a critic, you already have some bend toward God. You're looking for ways to engage with God through His Word or for strategies to help others do the same. Still you may not be quite clear on exactly why you want to do it or how to encourage others. Let's spend some time considering and answering the question, *Why read the Bible?* before we dive into some of the specifics of how, because the answers to how only matter if we've first answered the why.

WHY DO YOU WANT TO READ THE WHOLE BIBLE?

It's not just a heading here. This is a question for you: Why do *you* want to improve in Bible reading? Why, if this applies to you, do you want to read through the entire Bible?

How we answer this question matters. For many years, I wanted to read through the whole Bible because I thought I "should." I thought that's what "good Christians" did. My inner achiever certainly came to play, but down deep I also knew that if I was claiming to believe the Bible and the God of the Bible, I needed to actually read the Bible. I needed to know what it said for myself, not just bits and pieces of second-hand information. I tried to make this happen on my own because while I didn't have the term at the time, I was experiencing cognitive dissonance.

> *Cognitive dissonance is what happens in your brain when what you say doesn't match what you do.*

Cognitive dissonance is what happens in your brain when what you say doesn't match what you do. I said I believed that the whole Bible was absolutely true and that I should order my life by it, but my actions—not reading the whole thing—showed that I didn't fully believe it. I had a disconnect. My words and my actions didn't match, but after trying and failing enough times at reading the Bible I became accustomed to my cognitive dissonance and began rationalizing my behavior.

HABITUATING TO OUR SITUATION

We humans have a way of habituating to situations. In other words, we get used to things that we continually encounter. After long enough exposure, we stop seeing problems that we've become accustomed to. It's not unlike the Great Dane schmutz on some of the walls of my house. Because I live with a huge dog, I've become accustomed to that big nose occasionally leaving bits of food painted on the walls. I try to stay on top of it, but it's not my highest priority. After awhile I no longer see it; that is, until company comes over. It's then that I see the truth about my walls as I start noticing through the eyes of others what has become invisible to me.

When Alicia asked if I'd read through the whole Bible, the cognitive dissonance reached a fever pitch—I couldn't just kick the decision down the road any longer. It was time to deal with my rationalizations and excuses. I had the answer to my why. I no longer just wanted to read the whole Bible because I "should." God used Alicia's question to wake me up, to compel and propel me forward. I realized my own duplicity and my need for God to not only save me but to sanctify me. Up to that point, I thought I was in control. Through Alicia's question, God showed me Who was. When I found my answer to the question of why, the answer to my next question of how was not far behind.

So what is your answer to "Why do you want to read through the Bible?" Yes, you can write it down here:

If you left the space above blank, stick with me here for some Scriptural reasons that continue to drive me back into the Word of God, even on days when my grit and drive wane. If you already have a solid biblical answer to why and are eager to move to the how, you certainly can jump directly to the next chapter for the practical tips and strategies to get into God's Word faster because that, after all, is the entire point of this book. God's Word will do more for you than mine (or anyone else's for that matter) ever will. His Word trumps my word . . . every single time. That said, I'd love for you to stick with me for the next few pages as we go to Scripture for answers from God's Word itself as to why being in the Bible is crucial!

HELP WITH YOUR WHY

As I've mentioned, I've benefited by studying God's Word both deeply and widely. We can easily jump into small selections of Scripture and begin to go deep even when we have only a few minutes to spare, and I will take you to some passages that you can interact with more deeply as we consider this question.

To start off with, though, I need to take you wide across the pages of Scripture to give you a glimpse of a key recurring theme that spans the entire Book, a view that you can only see from the perspective of having read the whole.

A FLIGHT ABOVE ALASKA

Recently I flew (actually, was flown!) in a two-seater plane over a glacier in Alaska. I would do it again in a heartbeat, but I never would have opted-in to the first ride had I been asked. I speak in Alaska every couple of years, so when my friend Anita told me they scheduled me for a glacier fly over, I thanked her, forced a smile, and said a prayer. I didn't want to show fear, though it was rising in me. After all, these are people who will shoot a bear through a door and homestead through an Alaskan winter without the benefit of running water. I love these women and I trust them. So when they arranged for me to fly over a glacier, over the glacier I went and I saw with a stunning perspective that I'd never had in my countless other trips to state number 49. I didn't know what I had been missing!

Reading widely is like flying over a glacier. You see with a different perspective. There is beauty on the ground, but there is a different and complimentary beauty from above. Someone can tell you about it, you may see pictures of it, but nothing compares with seeing it for yourself. The same is true of the bird's eye perspective on the Word of God. That said, let me see if I can share just a bit from the wide perspective to help you catch a glimpse of what you can see fully for yourself as you begin to engage God through His Word.

THE BIBLE IS ABOUT RELATIONSHIP

From front to back, from first to last, the Bible is about relationship. While there are dos and don'ts, while there are laws and history and genealogies and geography, the Bible at its core is about relationship. It is not 80 hours of reading rules! Through the Bible God tells of His creation of mankind in relationship with Himself, mankind's severing the relationship, and God making the way through the incarnation, life, death, and resurrection of Jesus to restore that relationship.

> *From front to back, from first to last, the Bible is about relationship.*

The Bible starts in a garden where people are in relationship with God and it ends with a new heaven and new earth where people are brought back into the presence of God. Between the first creation and the time when all things are made new, God makes Himself known to the Israelites and to the peoples of the earth. God dwells among them in the tabernacle, in the temple, in the person of Jesus, and through His Spirit. The Bible, from cover to cover, chronicles God's movement toward man in relationship throughout history. It records in history and in words the life of the clearest revelation of all—Jesus Christ. As the author of Hebrews tells us, "God, after He spoke long ago to the fathers in the prophets, in many portions and in many ways, in these last days has spoken to us in His Son" (Hebrews 1:1).

In Romans, Paul argues that mankind can and does know much about God by simply looking around and paying attention (Romans 1:18ff), but that this kind of general revelation generally results in people suppressing truth. It is through special revelation that God reveals Himself in a salvific, that is saving, way. We read of His special revelation through the pages of Scripture.

If we want to know God, we cannot ignore His Word. He has spoken. If we believe that, we will listen and learn. We cannot live the Christian life apart from knowledge of God. We gain that knowledge of Him through His Word as His Spirit teaches us. For those who lament not "hearing from God," I have a question for you: Do you have a Bible? He has given me His Word, so who am I to neglect it? Again, as the author of Hebrews says, "How shall we escape if we neglect so great a salvation?" (2:1).

YOU CAN'T LIVE BY WHAT YOU DON'T KNOW

Relationships change us. When we walk in relationship with God we come to know Him and He changes us. We see this over and over in the Word of God. Noah walked with God. Abraham walked with God. David sought after God. Jesus calls His disciples to follow Him. Paul tells his readers to imitate him and follow him as he follows Christ.

We certainly engage with God through prayer, but the central way we walk in relationship with Him and learn to hear from Him is through His Word. We learn who He is, who we are in relationship to Him, what He has done for us, and how we can live in response to that through His Spirit who indwells us. For us to think we can follow God and live the Christian life without learning and pursuing Him through His Word when we have access to it is foolishness. I cannot live by what I do not know, nor can you.

Innately we know this, don't we? I can't play baseball without someone explaining the rules and showing me how to do it. I will not be good at it until I practice it. Why does the Cubs' Dansby Swanson have two Gold Glove awards? Because he knows the game of baseball and he practices it. He is a knower and a doer of baseball.

My daughter recently fell in love with the board game Wingspan and has become something of an evangelist for it. Because of this, the whole family has been learning how to play Wingspan. If you're a board game person, Wingspan would be the child if Settlers of Catan and Ticket to Ride were bred together around the theme of birds. It is a fun but

complex game. Unlike video games that prompt you at every step after
you start playing the game, you cannot wing it with Wingspan. You can't

> *You can't live by what
> you don't know.*

play it if you don't know it. The Christian life is similar. You can't live by what
you don't know.

But, you might say, what about the
Holy Spirit? Won't the Holy Spirit just tell me what to do? My answer:
What does the Word of God say? Let's survey two simple passages
together that are representative of many more.

HEAR, LOVE, TEACH

The first chapters of the Bible—Genesis, Exodus, Leviticus, and Numbers— introduce us to a God who interacts with people like Adam and
Eve, Abel, Enoch, Noah, Abraham, Isaac, Jacob, Joseph, and Moses to
name a few. As we come to the book of Deuteronomy, the fifth book of
the Bible and the final book of what is often referred to as the Torah or
the Books of Moses, we read of Moses giving God's instructions to the
people of Israel on how to walk in relationship with Him.

As Moses delivers these words to the people, they are at the end of a
forty-year wander in the wilderness after having been freed from a 400-
year captivity in Egypt. Situated in the land of Moab on the east side of the
Jordan River, Moses delivers God's words to the people who are about to
enter and possess the land God had promised to their forefather Abraham.

I'll lead you through some of the basics of Inductive Bible study
more specifically as we move further into this book, but let's dip our
toes into this method as we look at this passage. I've already told you the
historical situation of this passage and given you the basic context for
understanding. Let's look at this passage section by section to see if we
can discover some answers to the question of the *Why should I read and
study the Bible?* We'll start by praying.

> *Lord, please open our eyes to understand the words You spoke to the
> children of Israel through Moses and help us understand how we can
> apply them in our lives today.*

Take a moment to **READ** through Deuteronomy 6:4-9, pen in hand, and **CIRCLE** all of the verbs you notice. Verbs, of course, are action words like *hear, love, teach,* etc.

Deuteronomy 6:4-9

4   *"Hear, O Israel! The Lord is our God, the Lord is one!*

5   *"You shall love the Lord your God with all your heart and with all your soul and with all your might.*

6   *"These words, which I am commanding you today, shall be on your heart.*

7   *"You shall teach them diligently to your sons and shall talk of them when you sit in your house and when you walk by the way and when you lie down and when you rise up.*

8   *"You shall bind them as a sign on your hand and they shall be as frontals on your forehead.*

9   *"You shall write them on the doorposts of your house and on your gates."*

Take a moment and jot down the verbs you marked.

As Moses teaches the people about God, he begins by telling them to "Hear." They must hear who God is—"The Lord is our God, the Lord is one!" He then tells them that they are to "love" the Lord their God with their whole hearts. They are to respond to the truth of who God is with active, wholehearted love for Him.

God's words are to be on their hearts. When is the last time that something was "on your heart"? What was that last thing that you loved with "all your heart and with all your soul and with all your might"? What do you think about? Spend time on? Spend money on? Where do your resources and energies go? Go ahead and jot down your responses.

It is often said, "Show me your calendar and your bank account and I'll show you where your heart is." The God of the Bible does not want you to have a one-and-done Bible reading experience. He doesn't want you checking boxes with your hand when your heart is somewhere else. The Lord your God wants your heart . . . all of it. He wants a relationship with you.

According to Deuteronomy, He also wants you to know Him well enough and to know His Word intimately enough that you can pass it along to others . . . anytime and all the time! When does Moses tell the people to teach God's words to the next generation? He tells them to "talk of them when you sit in your house and when you walk by the way and when you lie down and when you rise up" (6:7). It's a Hebrew way of saying, "Do it all the time!"

Let's think through the logic of this. If you are to be able to teach specifically your kids or grandkids or more generally the next generation "all the time" what does that require of you? Of me? That's right. It requires that we know it ourselves to such an extent that we can pass it along. That's a tall order.

Let me ask you this: What is the one thing you could talk about for an hour straight if someone woke you up in the middle of the night? That likely is what is on your heart, what is part of your fiber. Maybe it's baseball, maybe it's how to make the best chocolate chip cookies on the planet, maybe it's something else. What if it were things of God and His Word?

As I write the chapter I'm weighing my time because I'm teaching a class on Romans tonight. Four hours writing today and then prep a little more for class. While I'm certainly prepping for the Romans class and have been all week because I want to present and foster the discussion as best I can with the specific folks who will be in the room—class management being a monster all its own—you could wake me in the middle of the night and we could talk Romans without any prep . . . because I've been prepping it my whole life.

29

One of the most memorable conversations in my life to date was the second one that I had with Jan Silvious, a writer and speaker friend of mine, who has been a long-time mentor to me. We met shortly after my first book was published. I was just discovering the connection between writing and speaking to support the writing, and I was not a fan! I've always loved to write, but speaking has been an acquired taste.

Anyway, I was Jan's "hostess" or "shadow" for a weekend conference in the Chicago area. My job was to bring her to the ballroom on time for each session, make sure she had water, and deliver her back to the airport on Sunday afternoon. As I was walking her to the ballroom to speak to about 700 women, I asked what her text was and she said something to the effect of, "I haven't quite decided yet." I don't remember too many things from that particular year of my life because I had little kids and was chronically sleep deprived, but I will never forget that. She answered like you'd answer the question "How do you want your steak prepared?" . . . "I don't know, medium, medium-well." She exuded cucumber-grade cool as she always does. I wanted to throw up as the stress overtook me for her!

What I didn't understand at the time was that she had been preparing for it all her life. She had multiple talks in her pocket. Squeeze her and Scripture oozed out. That's the picture we have with "when you rise up, and when you sit down, and when you walk along the way." Know it well enough so that it oozes out all the day.

The children of Israel were to love God with all their hearts, know His Word, and teach it to their children. They were to bind it to themselves and write it on their doorposts and gates.

As Moses continues we see why it will become so critically important. If you know some of the story already, you know that even when Israel was set apart and dwelled in God's presence with the tabernacle in their midst, seeing every day the pillar of cloud by day and the pillar of fire by night, they were notoriously disobedient even after witnessing God deliver them from Egypt with "a mighty hand and an outstretched arm" (Deuteronomy 26:8).

Moses tells the generation that will enter the land, most of whom were born in the wilderness, that they will face new challenges in the midst of the blessings. As you read Deuteronomy 6:10-15 note what benefits the people will receive in the land and what associated temptation they will also face. Go ahead and underline what God commands in verse 12 to combat the temptation.

Deuteronomy 6:10-15

10 "Then it shall come about when the LORD your God brings you into the land which He swore to your fathers, Abraham, Isaac and Jacob, to give you, great and splendid cities which you did not build,

11 and houses full of all good things which you did not fill, and hewn cisterns which you did not dig, vineyards and olive trees which you did not plant, and you eat and are satisfied,

12 then watch yourself, that you do not forget the LORD who brought you from the land of Egypt, out of the house of slavery.

13 "You shall fear only the LORD your God; and you shall worship Him and swear by His name.

14 "You shall not follow other gods, any of the gods of the peoples who surround you,

15 for the LORD your God in the midst of you is a jealous God; otherwise the anger of the LORD your God will be kindled against you, and He will wipe you off the face of the earth.

For 400 years the Israelites lived as slaves in the land of Egypt. Then they spent 40 years in, well, time-out in the wilderness on their way to the Promised Land. God cared for them. Their shoes did not wear out, but they spent 40 years with the same shoes. On coming into the land they would be blessed with plenty. These tent-dwelling wanderers would now have "houses full of good things" (6:11), a term which sounds strikingly familiar to many of us today. My goodness, I had to write myself

31

a study because my house filled up with far too many "good things." If that's you, too, check out *Bigger Barns: Living Content in a Material World*.

A temptation that they would face, and that most people who will pick up this book face, is forgetting God because we have plenty and are satisfied. Moses' words to the Israelites then echo in my ears today: "Watch yourself, that you do not forget the LORD." When our eyes shift from the Deliverer and Giver to the plenty and satisfaction, we're in trouble. The shiny things of life can turn our eyes away from the Giver of life!

As we continue with the rest of Deuteronomy 6, note what Moses says about the next generation in verse 20 and following. Go ahead and **UNDERLINE** the question the people are to prepare for.

Deuteronomy 6:16-25

16 *"You shall not put the LORD your God to the test, as you tested Him at Massah.*

17 *"You should diligently keep the commandments of the LORD your God, and His testimonies and His statutes which He has commanded you.*

18 *"You shall do what is right and good in the sight of the LORD, that it may be well with you and that you may go in and possess the good land which the LORD swore to give your fathers,*

19 *by driving out all your enemies from before you, as the LORD has spoken.*

20 *"When your son asks you in time to come, saying, 'What do the testimonies and the statutes and the judgments mean which the LORD our God commanded you?'*

21 *then you shall say to your son, 'We were slaves to Pharaoh in Egypt, and the LORD brought us from Egypt with a mighty hand.*

22 *'Moreover, the LORD showed great and distressing signs and wonders before our eyes against Egypt, Pharaoh and all his household;*

23 *He brought us out from there in order to bring us in, to give us the land which He had sworn to our fathers.'*

24 *"So the* LORD *commanded us to observe all these statutes, to fear the* LORD *our God for our good always and for our survival, as it is today.*

25 *"It will be righteousness for us if we are careful to observe all this commandment before the* LORD *our God, just as He commanded us.*

The people of Israel were to know the Lord their God and to be able to answer their children's questions about His Word. There's no speculation or guesswork involved. When their children ask, "What do the testimonies and the statutes and the judgments mean which the LORD our God commanded you?" they are to answer and tell what He has said and done. That requires knowing. That requires remembering. You can't live what you don't know.

NO GREATER SOURCE OF WISDOM

You may not be experiencing the cognitive dissonance that I felt. Perhaps you think you have enough "Bible" in you to adequately answer any question a 10-year old can pose. Maybe your why is still elusive. Let me add some pure pragmatism from Scripture that we find nestled in the middle of Psalm 119—the longest chapter in the Bible, weighing in at 176 verses.

Psalm 119 is an acrostic poem structured around the twenty-two letters of the Hebrew alphabet that declares the greatness of the Word of God. Nearly every line employs a synonym for God's Word (word, law, precept, statute, ordinance, judgment, or commandment). We'll look just at one of the stanzas, the Mem stanza (verses 97-104), that essentially claims God's Word to be of more benefit than the sum of every self-help book ever written!

As you read through the stanza, note who is being addressed and then **UNDERLINE** the benefits that the psalmist claims he has as a result of loving and meditating on God's revealed Word.

Psalm 119:97-104

97 *O how I love Your law!*
    It is my meditation all the day.

98 *Your commandments make me wiser than my enemies,*
    For they are ever mine.

99 *I have more insight than all my teachers,*
    For Your testimonies are my meditation.

100 *I understand more than the aged,*
    Because I have observed Your precepts.

101 *I have restrained my feet from every evil way,*
    That I may keep Your word.

102 *I have not turned aside from Your ordinances,*
    For You Yourself have taught me.

103 *How sweet are Your words to my taste!*
    Yes, sweeter than honey to my mouth!

104 *From Your precepts I get understanding;*
    Therefore I hate every false way.

The unnamed psalmist, likely David but possibly Ezra, makes stunning claims about the power of God's Word throughout Psalm 119, but nowhere—at least in my opinion—as pragmatically as in the Mem stanza.

The psalmist claims that because he loves and meditates on God's Word he is living a "more than" [Hebrew: *min*] life. He is not only wiser than his enemies, but also excels beyond two categories of people who should outpace him. Because of the Word of God, the psalmist has more insight than not just some, but *all of his teachers* and has more understanding than *the aged*.

If you've cracked a book to learn something that you don't know, if you've ever felt the sting of not understanding, this should make you take notice. True wisdom comes from God, the source of all wisdom. That, in fact, is what the psalmist declares as he proclaims to the Lord, "I

34

have not turned aside from your ordinances, for You Yourself have taught me" (v. 102).

Not only is the Word effective in providing wisdom and restraining evil, the psalmist claims that it is sweeter to his mouth than honey; if you ask me, the Word of God is sweeter than chocolate!

It's time to see for yourself!

DRAW NEAR THIS WEEK

As you go along throughout your week, pick one or both of these oppor-tunities for drawing near. Remember to ask God to give you a desire for His Word and move forward, trusting that He will answer you.

- Start or continue reading the Gospel of John to help you begin building the habit of daily fixing your eyes on Jesus.
- Read Psalm 119 and note for yourself the benefits associated with knowing and living God's Word. Be aware it will take about 20 minutes to read this single psalm.

DISCUSS TOGETHER

These questions can be used in a discussion group if you're using this book in a Bible study setting or book club. You can also use them to process through what you're learning on your own.

- What has been your why for reading the Bible in the past?
  - How has that worked?
- Has your why going forward changed at all as you've been considering the importance of reading?
  - If so, what has changed?
- Have you ever experienced cognitive dissonance with regard to your Bible reading? How have you dealt with that?

READ Deuteronomy 6 aloud and discuss:

- What did Moses call on the people to do in verses 4-9?
  - How were their hearts to be involved?
  - How does your heart's current condition compare?
  - What effect would obedience have on their children?
  - What would it take for you to be prepared to speak "all the day" of the things of the Lord?
- What situation does Moses address in verses 10-15?
  - What temptation will the people face?
  - How are they to stand in the face of it?
  - How are you doing with similar temptations? Why?
- What future day does Moses talk about in verses 16-25?
  - What question was coming for Israel?
  - Are you prepared to answer similar questions?

READ Psalm 119:97-104 aloud and discuss:

- What did you learn about the Word of God in the Mem stanza of Psalm 119?
- How did the psalmist engage the Word of God?
- What benefits did the psalmist experience as a result?
- If you were to experience similar benefits, how would that affect your life?

READ TOGETHER

If you're meeting with a group, spend some of your time reading the Bible aloud. Typically, you'll take turns with each person reading a chapter. Again, if you have a larger group, break up into smaller groups of no more than five people each. Always remember to give people the opportunity to participate through listening as others read.

This week read **Psalm 119,** alternating readers with each stanza. It should take you about 20 minutes. As you read, watch for the benefits associated with knowing and living the Word. Some people may have chosen to read this during the week—and that's great! With each reading it will continue to unfold more and more.

When you are finished, pray for one another asking that you will have the desire to know God through His Word and that He will guide you with the specifics of how you can overcome any barriers that currently stand in your way.

CHAPTER 3

The Why and How of Going Wide

Simple Strategies for Reading Wide

AT MY STAGE IN LIFE, I could pick a new reading plan every year for the rest of my life and not run out even given my family's history of producing nonagenarians (aka 90 year olds!). Dearth of plans is not the problem; the ability to live within strict plans is the issue for most of us who are plan-averse.

Whether you're generally distractible, drop-dead busy, hate being in someone else's box, or something else, you're likely here with me because plans have failed both of us. We need something else. We need enough structure to keep us on the road, but not so much that we suffocate. So if you're a plan person, consider yourself excused to go follow your plan and read, but know that you are still welcome to come along on this journey as the tools you'll learn here will likely help you with someone along the way who just doesn't fit into traditional programmed approaches to Bible reading.

At my church, our pastor often refers to our congregation as the island of misfit toys. It's an apt description of all groups of people in a way, I think. We all need Jesus, we all need the Word, but not everyone flourishes with a three-chapter a day program that resets on January 1 every year. I don't know about you, but what I need is something simple, something enjoyable, and something sustainable. Learning to go deep and wide in the Word and not try to gut it out by myself has worked for me and many others. I think it will work for you, too!

> *We all need Jesus, we all need the Word, but not everyone flourishes with a three-chapter a day program that only resets on January 1.*

TRIES AND FAILS

It's my guess that if you already have a few tries and fails under your belt, you've probably started adopting and tending to several lies that have grown under your care and continue to block you in your reading journey. Lies are pervasive and myriad, so this is certainly not an exhaustive list, but see if you've bought into any of these common lies about Bible reading that I've fought over the years:

- I have to start at the beginning.
- I have to understand everything right away.
- I don't have the time.
- I have to stick to a strict schedule.
- I just can't do it.

Maybe you relate with one of them. Maybe you relate with all! Likely you have others to add. We live in a culture of lies and we will need to fight against some very specific lies to make it through the Bible.

Don't worry, we'll address these as well as others from various angles as we walk through the sections on reading widely and studying deeply. We'll look at another pervasive lie that we fall for when we get to the Go Together section, but you'll have to keep reading!

As we do this, the strategy that we'll be following is to **go wide** in the Word, to **go deep** in the Word, and to **go together** on our journey!

WHAT LIES HAVE YOU BELIEVED?

It's possible that even now you're believing the lie or a variant of a lie that says if you find the "right resource" to tell you about the Bible, that you'll have a magic bullet of some sort and that you won't have to do the hard work yourself. This book is not your magic bullet. No book is.

This book is not your magic bullet. No book is.

You certainly can learn about the Bible from gifted teachers. I've benefited over the years from pastors, professors, and gifted teachers like Kay Arthur (founder of Precept Ministries) who has taught people around the world how to study the Bible. Teachers can give you facts and frameworks, but even if they could give you all of the facts, as middlemen they cannot give you what you need from the Bible—time learning from God Himself. The best teachers will equip you to study, to mine the treasures of God's Word for yourself. They will teach you how to study and how to think and let the Word and the Spirit renew your mind.

SEEING THE TRUTH FOR YOURSELF

Think about it this way: having been to Maui, I can tell you much about the island. I can explain to you the beauty, the climate, and something of the culture. I can describe the miles of beachfront and the mesmerizing sunsets. I can show you pictures, videos even of the scenery and the people. I can bring you bits of sand, a mug, and send postcards. I can tell you all about Maui, but until you set foot there, you will not know it. The same is true of the Bible. You can learn all of the facts, but until you immerse yourself in the living Word, you will never know the wonder. And make no mistake, you can know many facts without knowing the wonder of the Word for yourself.

And so, as we journey together, I will be passing along some facts that I hope will make reading a little easier and more accessible to you, but I cannot do the heavy lifting for you. If I could, I would, but the best I can do is be your guide and enthusiastic cheerleader to exhort you to read God's Word for yourself and through the witness of the Holy Spirit to know the One True God and Jesus Christ Whom He has sent!

THE CHALLENGE OF READING WIDELY

For many people who long to love and read the Bible, something has short-circuited that goal. If that is you, be assured that you are not alone. The Bible can be a tough book to grasp and it is long. You know this. Although authored by God whose message is consistent, the Bible was at the same time written through various human authors. Thus, while the message is consistent throughout, different human authors have different styles and stress different concepts, thereby adding complexity.

As you begin to study deeply, the broad reading you do will make more sense because you will come to understand in a more thorough way the concepts that run through all of the Bible. At the same time, the more widely you read, the more sense you will be able to make of individual passages because you will have better understanding of the larger context.

The combination of reading widely and studying deeply will propel you in your understanding of God's Word. While people often tend toward one or the other, reading widely and studying deeply synergize and multiply our efforts. All of this, of course, is by the power of the Holy Spirit—nothing positive gets done in the spiritual realm apart from Him!

WHY READ WIDE?

Reading widely helps us in several significant ways.

1. READING WIDELY GIVES US THE BIG PICTURE AND THE GENERAL LAY OF THE LAND.

At the most basic level, if we don't understand the problem of sin, we don't understand the need for the cross. We gain an understanding of who God is as we look at how He has revealed Himself over time. In this we also become more comfortable interacting with the Bible because we come to know the lay of the land.

Think for a moment of how different it is to drive around your hometown than it is to drive in a new state or country. Driving when you don't know where you are, even aided by a GPS, is unnerving at best. As we learn to read widely, we learn to relax a bit more into the Word and the process of pursuing God through it.

2. READING WIDELY PROVIDES THE NEEDED FOUNDATION FOR STUDYING DEEPLY.

Deep study of the Word, which we'll talk about soon, depends on context. Reading widely provides us the context we need to understand the biblical narrative. Good biblical interpretation depends on understanding context. The full context in Bible study is the whole Book. We pick and choose at our own peril.

3. READING WIDELY HELPS CONNECT THE HEAD AND THE HEART.

I am speaking experientially here, but check if this is not true in your life, too. When I lock into an exclusively deep-study mode, I have a tendency to see a head-heart disconnect. If I'm focused on parsing verbs or analyzing the text of Scripture exclusively, I find that I can fall into a season of spiritual drought. Is deep study important? Absolutely! 100%! But if I continually force literature that was meant to be communicated as longer narratives into microscopic slides, there will be loss. If I try to control the text rather than submit to it, I'm looking for trouble. If I don't read the New Testament letters as letters and proceed at a verse a day pace, I will miss out.

To be sure, slowing the bus down also yields massive fruit, but not in isolation. Lest you think I'm tossing the baby of memorizing and meditating out with the bath water, trust me: I am not. We'll address those later.

I've found that when I focus on the Word in an exclusively deep and academic way, there is a sense in which I am trying to control the text, but when I read widely alongside my deep study I allow it to work in and master me. Think about it.

4. READING WIDELY BRINGS REST AND JOY.

I am again speaking experientially here. While exegesis (drawing the meaning out of the text) and hermeneutics (the art and science of interpreting Scripture) pay massive dividends, they involve a level of striving, good striving for sure, beneficial seeking after God, but striving nonetheless. Reading widely, sometimes simply listening to the Word, brings me rest and joy that can elude me when I have to "produce" to feed others. If you're in teaching ministry on any level, you know what I mean.

WHAT I AM NOT SAYING . . .

- I am not saying deep study is not important. It absolutely is, and we'll talk about that in the next section.
- I am not saying that slowing to the point of memorizing and meditating is not important. It also absolutely is, and we'll cover that along with deep study!

DON'T LOSE YOUR FIRST LOVE

While memorizing—both as a child and as an adult—has probably been the single most significant piece of my spiritual growth, nothing brings me greater joy than reading God's Word widely. As important as deep study of God's Word is—and it is critical—study to the exclusion of reading widely and simply enjoying God in relationship can lead to a first-love loss similar to that of the Ephesians (see Revelation 2:1-7) who in spite of solid theology were reprimanded by the risen Christ.

As a long-time inductive study leader and trainer I often encounter true Jesus lovers who need to be reminded of their first love. I've seen

Pencils have their time and place, but their time and place is not everywhere, all the time.

and I've experienced how all-study-all-the-time can lead to a head-heart disconnect. Again, study is critical—Paul writes in 2 Timothy 2:15, "Study to show yourself approved unto God"—but along with study we need to learn how to take a breath, put the pencil down, and simply enjoy reading the Bible and spending time with the Lord. Pencils have their time and place, but their time and place is not everywhere, all the time.

TIPS AND STRATEGIES FOR READING WIDE

So let's jump in with some almost too-practical tips for reading God's Word widely that have helped me navigate my way through the Bible repeatedly over the years. By laying these out in snippets, I hope to make this book scannable and skimmable so that you can find what is helpful without being bogged down by simple principles that you already know. Nothing that I write is an end in itself; I write to direct you to the Word of God and not my own.

My goal with all of my writing is to propel you into God's Word as efficiently and effectively as possible. Growth is not a one-size-fits-all proposition. While we grow in fits and spurts in different ways and at different times, all true growth roots in the Spirit and the Word. This is my attempt to show you some strategies that have helped me on the path. As with fish, eat the meat and spit out any bones that may remain.

GO WIDE STRATEGY
Pray Before You Start and Pray as You Go

We've talked about asking God for the desire to read, and we've talked about the truth that in the Word of God, God Himself teaches us. Still, it is easy to fall into old habits of trying to read on our own power. Each time you begin to read or study, remember to pray that God would lead you and teach you! Remember, His Spirit is the One who leads His disciples into all truth (John 16:13).

Try Starting with 1 Samuel

If you've been a Christian for any length of time, chances are you've had at least a measure of success in reading some New Testament books. For most people the Old Testament seems like the highest mountain to scale. Just looking at the numbers, it's about three times as long as the New Testament. Add to that it contains Leviticus, Ezekiel, and Job. It is also home to the longest chapter in the Bible, Psalm 119, which is longer than several New Testament books! Because of its size, we need to start gaining a level of comfort in reading the Old Testament early on so we don't change our mind on the idea of reading through the Bible and bail!

The book of 1 Samuel is a wonderful place to start, particularly if you have some working knowledge of the general biblical storyline. It reads like a story and is not nearly as long as the early books of the Bible. While it is 31 chapters, they are relatively short chapters (average of 26 verses per chapter) and the narrative moves along. Beginning with the account of Hannah, the mother of the prophet Samuel as she cries out to God for a son, the book of 1 Samuel also tells of the life of Saul, Israel's first king, of David and Goliath, and the continual pursuit of David by Saul.

The first time I read through the Bible successfully I started in 1 Samuel. While I believe God led me to that starting point, let me share with you a few reasons it was particularly good for me and may also be for you. The book of 1 Samuel is straight-up narrative with an engaging storyline that pulls you forward across chapter breaks. The narrative continues essentially uninterrupted through the end of Second Kings.

Because I had a background in the biblical storyline, I knew the basics of what was happening in Genesis as well as the narrative portions of Exodus and Numbers. I was also familiar with the story of the conquest of the land in Joshua and the accounts of the Judges.

The first time I read through the Bible successfully I started in 1 Samuel.

While familiar to me, the books of 1 and 2 Samuel and the Kings provided much "newer" content and kept me engaged. I also had a clear path forward as I was getting started. Sure, starting from the beginning gives you a clear path, but the path that goes from the end of Exodus through the first half of Numbers is straight uphill!

GO WIDE STRATEGY

Don't Start in Genesis

If you've tried and failed before, don't start in Genesis! You've read Genesis, probably more than once, right? As Westerners we always start at the left and read to the right. We open on page one and march forward. We mock people who turn to the back of the book to see how it is going to end. If you want to read through the Bible and not just read excerpts, it makes logical sense to begin in Genesis. I get that. It is the approach most people take.

The reason I recommend not starting in Genesis is because most people who will pick up this book have already read Genesis in one or more (often many!) failed attempts to read through the Bible using a conventional approach. Genesis is great reading, but it is long and for most people a continual review of what they've already read—50 chapters. If you've already read Genesis, give yourself credit for that book and start further in where it is harder to measure how far you *haven't* read.

I know it sounds shallow, but most people need to see progress and feel a sense of momentum to help them continue toward a goal. Putting a bookmark five pages into a 2000-page book can be downright demoralizing. It's often said that the definition of insanity is doing the same thing over and over again and expecting different results. If you already have a history of starting and failing in Genesis, be sane and start somewhere else!

> *It's often said that the definition of insanity is doing the same thing over and over again and expecting different results. If you already have a history of starting and failing in Genesis, be sane and start somewhere else!*

If you start further in, you'll feel like you're making progress faster and be more inclined to keep going. The other problem with starting in Genesis is that even if you do make it through the book relatively quickly, you'll be tempted to continue on in a linear fashion and will soon find out how hard it is to read the end of Exodus, all of Leviticus, and the beginning of Numbers consecutively. Let's say you do crush those and head on toward the "easy-reading" historical books; you will eventually hit the wall which I affectionately call Isaiahjeremiahlamentationsezekiel. Look long? That's because it is!

Sure, Lamentations is only five chapters, but have you done a page count on the other three lately? They're good when they're taken in portions, but try to swallow them whole and you'll likely choke. At least I do. Maybe the spiritual giants among us can cruise through these in succession, but I don't suggest it. I like to take the prophets in smaller portions and mixed in along the way with some easier reading. Shallow? Again, probably. I'll own that, but knowing and identifying where I will likely fail in a read-through has helped me to adapt and successfully read the entire Bible many times in many translations over the now many years of my life.

THERE'S ALWAYS AN EXCEPTION!

If you're horrified by the "Don't Start in Genesis" tip, it's possible that you're an exception. Here are a couple of exceptions to my general "rule."

Exception #1: If you do not have any background in the stories of the Bible from Sunday school as a child or other teaching along the way and you have no frame of reference for the basic biblical accounts of Creation, Adam and Eve, Noah, Abraham, Isaac, Jacob, Joseph, and the Exodus, go ahead and start in Genesis. People who reach adulthood with no biblical background are becoming more and more common as the United States has become a post-Christian nation. If this is you, get the foundation in Genesis and the first part of Exodus. You can continue with the "through storyline"—reading the text that moves the narrative forward—of the Old Testament by following the outline on the next page.

Exception #2: If you have been a strictly New Testament reader and have been too timid to *ever* venture into the Old Testament, go ahead and start in Genesis. You'll find engaging narrative, the foundational accounts of creation, sin, the flood, and the beginnings of God's dealings with His chosen people. Genesis is the book of beginnings. If you find yourself wanting to continue marching straight forward, I'd recommend on the first pass to stick with the through-storyline without being drawn into additional details that often stymie reading progress. In doing this, you can learn the main storyline of Scripture and come back later to pick up the more detailed accounts of how to build a tabernacle (the end of Exodus), the specifics of Hebrew law (Leviticus), the census of the Hebrew people (the beginning of Numbers), and words of the prophets.

GO WIDE STRATEGY

New to Bible Reading? Start with Jesus

If you're new to the faith or simply exploring a relationship with Jesus, the New Testament Gospel accounts are a great place to start your

THE **THROUGH STORYLINE** OF THE OLD TESTAMENT

- ☐ Genesis
- ☐ Exodus 1–20, 24, 32–34
- ☐ Leviticus 10, 26
- ☐ Numbers 11–14, 16–17, 20–25, 27, 31–32
- ☐ Deuteronomy 1–11, 27–34
- ☐ Joshua 1–9, 22–24
- ☐ Judges
- ☐ Ruth
- ☐ 1 Samuel
- ☐ 2 Samuel
- ☐ 1 Kings 1–4, 8–22
- ☐ 2 Kings
- ☐ Daniel 1–6
- ☐ Lamentations
- ☐ Ezra
- ☐ Esther
- ☐ Nehemiah

time in the Word. Matthew, Mark, Luke, and John each record the life, ministry, death, and resurrection of Jesus from slightly different perspectives with distinct original readership in mind. Any of them will provide a great starting place for a new believer or interested truth seeker to spend time and consider Jesus. Here's a little more info on each that may be helpful as you decide where to start.

Scholars refer to Matthew, Mark, and Luke as the synoptic Gospels (*synoptic* meaning "one view") because of their similar way of recounting information. John is the outlier as he organizes his Gospel account around seven major signs that Jesus performed.

Reading times shown in the following paragraphs are on average from Crossway Publishers.[4]

MATTHEW

Matthew, Jesus' disciple who was also referred to as Levi, writes to a primarily Jewish audience and presents Jesus as the fulfillment of Old Testament prophecy being both the Son of Abraham and the Son of David. (28 chapters: 2h, 21m)

MARK

Mark, likely John Mark of Acts 12:12, pens Peter's words regarding the life of Jesus. This Gospel was geared to a more Roman audience and it is the shortest of the Gospel accounts. (16 chapters: 1h, 23m)

LUKE

Luke, the beloved physician and ministry associate of Paul, writes about the life and ministry of Jesus with a Greek audience in mind. He specifically addresses the account to a reader he calls "Theophilus." Luke records eyewitness reports of those who walked with Jesus, having himself investigated carefully. Although "shorter" than Matthew at 24 chapters, Luke is actually a longer text as he is more chatty. (24 chapters: 2h, 24m)

JOHN

Written by the beloved disciple, John tells his purpose for writing in the later verses of his account saying, "Therefore many other signs Jesus also performed in the presence of the disciples, which are not written in this book; but these have been written so that you may believe that Jesus is the Christ, the Son of God; and that believing you may have life in His name" (John 20:30-31). (21 chapters: 1h, 51m)

---

4. Crossway. Infographic: You have more time for Bible reading than you think. November 19, 2018. https://www.crossway.org/articles/infographic-you-can-read-more-of-the-bible-than-you-think/

GO WIDE STRATEGY
Have Some Cookies!

For additional help in reading through the whole Bible, check out *Cookies on the Lower Shelf*. In three courses of ten weeks each, I'll walk you through Scripture with questions that will help you reason through the text and apply what you're learning as you go! *Cookies on the Lower Shelf* puts Bible reading within reach! The title of the series comes from a saying my grandpa always used. He was a pastor and always taught in such a way as to "put the cookies on the lower shelf" so that the good things of God were accessible to everyone!

GO WIDE STRATEGY
Navigate Wide With Your Table of Contents

Complex reading systems work for some people. From time to time I run into a person who can manage a system that involves daily readings from both the Old and New Testaments. Others can power through the simple three chapters a day to infinity and beyond. Maybe I'm an outlier, but neither of those approaches have worked for me. Too much complexity frustrates me, and too much rigidity (those three chapters a day) discourages me because I inevitably break routine—either over or under!

My guess is that you don't work well in systems or you wouldn't be reading this book! For most of us, the more complex the system, the less chance we'll make it because of the "I Missed a Day" principle if nothing else. Ever notice how hard it is to catch up when you miss a day on a schedule . . . any schedule? If the washing machine doesn't run when it's supposed to or the dishes slide by for more than one meal without being addressed, the resulting problem is more than the sum of its parts.

I hosted a houseful of college students this past weekend. It's Friday morning and I'm still looking at several loads of sheets and towels that need to be washed before I'm back to normal! Two days ago, I was thinking about buying a second washing machine. The additional laundry volume seemed overwhelming because you can only run so many loads in a day. Load size, number of loads, plus washer run time. It's math.

Same thing when you're dealing with a strict Bible reading schedule. When you miss a day, or heaven forbid you have an emergency that throws you off schedule for multiple days, the tendency is to want to do a catch-up every time. This works if you catch up quickly. Problems mount when you're trying to catch up for a few misses all at once. Instead of "having" to read three chapters a day, all of a sudden you're looking at six, nine, twelve, or more. Add to that the guilt of looking at what we haven't done. Maybe that's just me . . . "I should be 'there' by now, but I'm only 'here.'" Ouch.

In my estimation, complex schedules move us squarely into the academic realm, and not the good academic realm. When my eyes see the word "schedule," my soul sees the word "syllabus," and the relational aspect of the activity plummets. We find ourselves in "have to" land instead of "get to" land. It's the same material, but with a dangerous shift in mindset.

To decrease the complexity, pick a book and finish it before you move on to another. Then track your progress simply and efficiently with a penciled checkmark in your table of contents. I know, you may be thinking, "What if I get lost in the middle of Leviticus or Ezekiel? What then?" Take a breath. We'll get there. :)

GO WIDE STRATEGY

Find the Right Translation

Did you know that there are approximately 900 English translations of the Bible, according to the American Bible Society?[5] Yes, I was shocked by this number, too! Let's narrow our discussion to the top sellers in 2023 of members of the Evangelical Christian Publishers Association.[6]

---

5. American Bible Society. Number of English translations of the Bible. December 2, 2009. https://news.americanbible.org/article/number-of-english-translations-of-the-bible

6. ReadGoodBooks. ECPA Bible translations bestsellers: best of 2023. https://christianbookexpo.com/bestseller/translations.php?id=BO23

Top Selling Bible Translations

1. New International Version
2. King James Version
3. English Standard Version
4. New Living Translation
5. Christian Standard Version
6. New King James Version
7. Reina Valera (Spanish Translation)
8. New International Reader's Version
9. New American Standard Bible
10. New Revised Standard Version

There was a day not long ago when the only option for English readers was the original King James Version of the Bible, first published in 1611. Most of us, even if we haven't read that translation, are aware that it reads like Shakespeare. Many in the over-50 crowd who think that reading the Bible is just too hard have had a try-and-fail with King James. The King James Version of the Bible served the church well for many years, particularly for those who lived when what we refer to as "Old English" was the common language of the day.

Today we have a variety of choices in translation, some of which are exceptionally easy to read. While I am a stickler for word-for-word translations in Bible study—New American Standard, English Standard, or New King James—the readability in other translations can be helpful when trying to read the Bible through.

Bear in mind, however, the more easy a translation is to understand, the more power you've given to the translator to tell you what the text means. Two translations that hit a nice middle path, staying true to the original languages yet making the reading as easy as possible are the New International Version and the Christian Standard Version. My favorite

Bible for all things is the New American Standard, 1995 edition, but I may be a Bible nerd.

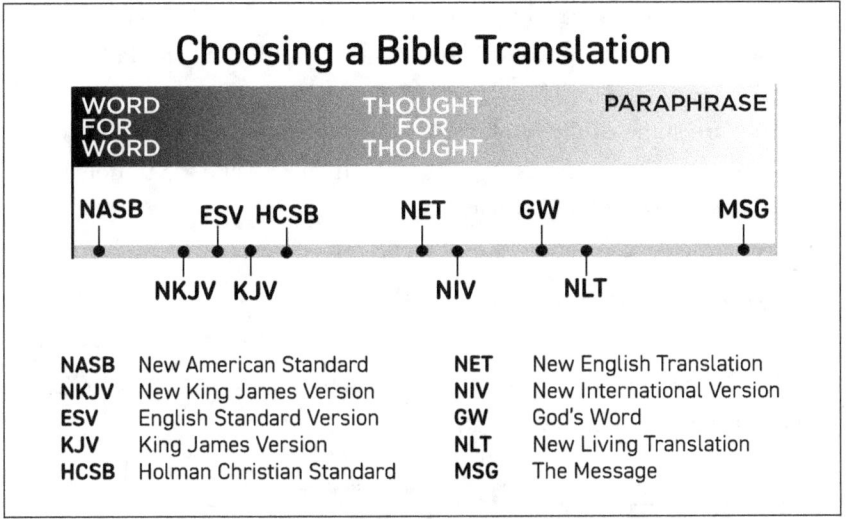

Choosing a Bible Translation

WORD FOR WORD	THOUGHT FOR THOUGHT	PARAPHRASE

NASB   ESV HCSB   NET   GW   MSG

NKJV KJV   NIV   NLT

NASB	New American Standard	**NET**	New English Translation
NKJV	New King James Version	**NIV**	New International Version
ESV	English Standard Version	**GW**	God's Word
KJV	King James Version	**NLT**	New Living Translation
HCSB	Holman Christian Standard	**MSG**	The Message

GO WIDE STRATEGY

Read in "Chunks"

Slow and steady may win the race, but reading a couple of minutes a day is not how we read most books. So why should we read the Bible any differently? One of the best ways to connect with what you are reading is to set aside a couple of hours and just get at it. Think about how hard it is to be swept into a novel when you only let yourself read one page. The same is true with the Bible. So much of the Bible is narrative, and narrative does not lend itself to ten-minute reads. You'll be amazed at what God will do if you simply set aside some extended time to spend alone with Him in His Word. Certainly you can't do this every day, but you sure can regularly with a little planning. I suggest a two-hour chunk, but even thirty focused minutes will start to propel you on your way.

This is an especially good idea if you're just starting out with a serious reading program. Take the time to immerse yourself in the Word and to rid yourself of the fear that you can't do it. When you get right down to it, isn't that half the problem, the fear that you'll start and fail . . . again?

Here are some of the books I like to read when I'm "chunk" reading:

- Historical books: Genesis; Joshua and Judges; 1 and 2 Samuel; 1 and 2 Kings; Ezra and Nehemiah
- Prophetic books: Daniel and Revelation
- Any of the gospels (Matthew, Mark, Luke, or John)
- The book of Acts

Reading in chunks also helps us to stop looking at the clock. What is it about a clock that is so fascinating anyway?

GO WIDE STRATEGY

When You Read Genesis, Pay Attention to the Players!

When you eventually read Genesis, you will enjoy it! In it we learn the origin stories of mankind in general and the people of Israel in specific. In addition to God Himself, Adam, Noah, Abraham, Isaac, Jacob, and Joseph are the headliners without a doubt.

Genesis, though, also provides us with the origin stories of many of the nations surrounding Israel that will show up throughout the biblical text as relatives, enemies, and allies. When we pay attention to first mentions in Genesis, we set ourselves up to understand later encounters between Israel and the surrounding nations, most of whom are distant cousins! This will set the foundation for reading both the historical and prophetic books of the Old Testament. The prophets are hard enough when you know who the players are, so pay attention in Genesis and you'll thank yourself later. Also, realize you won't do it perfectly! That's okay. Just pay attention and you will pick it up little by little.

I'll give you some of the highlights here so you'll have a leg up. You'll actually learn them in a way that will stick when you read their stories in context! I like to think of these in terms of friends and enemies. When you read about other people and nations, consider how they came about and how they relate to God's working with His people and in the process of salvation history.

The "**...ites**" of the Bible			
	person of origin		nation/people group
Lot's sons	Moab		**Moabites**
	Ben-Ammi		**Ammonites**
Abraham's son (son of promise)	Isaac	Jacob	**Israelites**
		Esau	**Edomites**
Abraham's "other" sons (from Hagar and Keturah)	Ishmael (by Hagar)		**Ishmaelites**
	Midian (by Keturah)		**Midianites**

Other notables as you go along through Scripture will be the Amalekites, the Philistines, the Egyptians, the people of Tyre and Sidon, the Babylonians, and the Assyrians.

When you know the origin stories or at least are aware of first mentions, it's easier to connect when people and people groups continue to resurface throughout Scripture.

Think about it. Knowing how people connect makes a difference. I grew up in a church that had a family with eleven sons, the Leafblads. The joke was that if you stayed around long enough, eventually you would be related to a Leafblad. My Leafblad is my sister-in-law. You could literally draw a family tree and see all of the shirttail relatives throughout the church. Life is just more interesting when you know how everyone fits together, isn't it?!

One of these days, perhaps I'll release *Friends & Enemies,* a Bible study on how all of the nations around Israel relate to her. Yes, I've written it, but it is lost on a hard drive somewhere. Seriously. Truth is, with this information, you don't actually need the study. You can do this on your own by making that simple list and paying attention! Once you understand the relationship of each of the countries to Israel, you'll have smooth sailing!

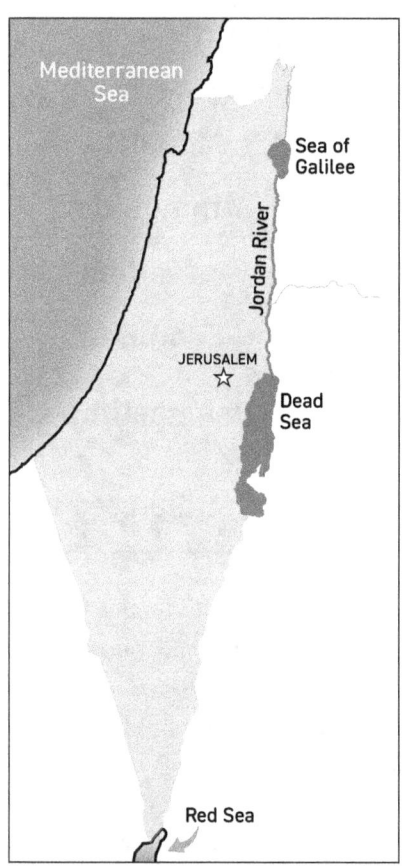

Use a Simple Map

When you read location words without being able to attach them to an actual place, they become essentially meaningless. As you read, keep your bearings with a simple map and remember that Israel is the size of the state of New Jersey! Here's one to get you started.

Why Biblical Geography Makes You Feel Stupid

There's a reason that biblical geography makes us all feel stupid at one time or another. We think, "Seriously, if Israel is only the size of New Jersey, why can't I get the hang of the geography?" There's a simple reason.

Time. Those of us who live in the United States—most of my readers
I'm assuming—know an essentially static map. Chicago has always been
Chicago, New York always New York in our lifetimes. When we deal with
biblical geography, we are dealing with a small piece of land over a great
deal of time where location names change . . . repeatedly. Yeah.

GO WIDE STRATEGY

Know the Five Bodies of Water

Learning the five bodies of water in and near Israel will give you a simple
framework for understanding where events take place. The first three
(mercifully) can be recalled with a rhyme: Med Sea, Dead Sea, Red Sea.

Med Sea (Great Sea) — The Mediterranean Sea, referred to in the biblical text as the Great Sea, is the western border of the land of Israel.
[WEST]

Dead Sea (Salt Sea) — Known to us as the Dead Sea, this is usually
referred to in the Bible as the Salt Sea, the Sea of the Plain (or Arabah,
"plain" in Hebrew), or the Eastern Sea. The Dead Sea is on the eastern
border of Israel at the base of the Jordan River. [SOUTHEAST]

Red Sea — Although scholars debate the exact location of the crossing,
the Red Sea associated with the book of Exodus is to the south and west
of the Promised Land near Egypt. [SOUTHWEST]

Sea of Galilee (Sea of Tiberias, Lake of Gennesaret, Lake Kinneret) — To
English speakers, the Sea of Galilee is a misnomer as it is actually a fresh-
water lake. Located in the northeastern part of the Promised Land, this
storied lake appears often in the narratives about Jesus. The Jordan River
flows through this body of water. [NORTHEAST]

Jordan River — The Jordan River divides the main section of the Promised Land from the trans-Jordan region where the descendants of Reu-
ben, Gad, and half of the tribe of Manasseh eventually settled (yes, I'm

probably getting ahead of myself). This is the eastern border of modern Israel. [EAST]

Drop the Pencil

Let's talk about pencils. If you're an academic of any sort, I'm guessing that you like your pencils, pens, and highlighters. I sure do. I still have some old college textbooks hanging around and I chuckle when thumbing through them because I underlined and/or highlighted more of the text than not. Marking a text takes time. It's one of the reasons that inductive Bible study uses marking as part of the process because it slows people down.

Assuming you like to mark up textbooks and other non-fiction reads, consider for a moment how you approach a novel. Do you underline and highlight and jot notes in the margins of novels? Now I know in recent years that high school teachers have students annotating their novels in freshman literature class, but most of us when we're reading for pleasure do not mark or annotate.

I just finished re-reading the *Brothers Karamazov* (I still don't like the ending!) and the only marks that I made in the text were to help keep me from forgetting who certain characters were along the way. You'll increase your reading speed and forward momentum if you can manage to drop the pencil while you're reading the Bible widely. Pick it up for sure when you're studying deeply—we'll talk about that in upcoming chapters—but when reading widely resist the urge to mark (or at least the urge to over-mark!) and allow yourself to see the forest instead of nosing up to the bark of every tree.

Before you discount this tip, please hear this. The first time that I was able to read through the whole Bible this—along with not starting in Genesis—was the biggest strategic change I made. I have since read through multiple translations of the Bible (some favorites multiple times) over the years and use the pencil sparingly, particularly to note connections between passages that continue to surface more and more as I read the whole narrative and not just bits here and there. I mark with vigor when I'm studying specific passages deeply, but I've learned to rule my tools in this area so I can gain context more efficiently and effectively.

GO WIDE STRATEGY

Use an Audio Bible

One of my favorite tools for reading the text of Scripture widely is an audio Bible. We've come a long ways since the days of the Bible on 48 cassette tapes or 79 compact discs. Listening to the Bible used to be a cumbersome task. Now anyone who has access to this book likely also has access to the Bible in a digital format at their fingertips. Some of you are now thinking, "But listening doesn't 'count.'" I get it. I tell myself that lie sometimes, too.

But the truth is, it does count. Paul tells us in Romans 10:17 that "... faith comes from hearing, and hearing by the word of Christ." I know, you're right that you won't learn in the same way by listening to the text of Scripture, but you will still learn. You will also be more inclined to begin to memorize the Word particularly if you listen to it more often.

The difference in hearing someone else read or in listening in a version that differs from your typical Bible translation may also alert you to passages of the text that you tend to read over due to familiarity. On more than one occasion, I've had to push pause and compare the audio with the written because a different translation has landed on my ears in a way I had never "heard" before.

I often listen to an audio Bible while on my exercise bike. I've found that it takes about 20 hours to listen to the New Testament which is a perfect benchmark for a month's worth of exercise—when I'm in a good exercise space at least.

An audio Bible can also provide a much-needed boost when you're having trouble making it through harder passages. Following along in your physical Bible while someone else reads to you can be a lifesaver when the names in a genealogy trip you up or laws seem overwhelming. When you're reading on your own, you can start to think, "How long will this take? Will I ever get through this?" When you work through a passage with an audio Bible, you can look at the run time and realize that in the time it would take to watch an average movie, you can listen through the whole book of Leviticus. Buy yourself a mocha and follow along if and when the going gets tough.

My favorite audio Bibles are *The Word of Promise* app and *The Bible Experience,* but I hear about more of them every day, it seems. *The Word of Promise* dramatizes the New King James Version of the Bible. It features Jim Caviziel (Jesus in the *Passion of the Christ*) as Jesus and a cast of 600 actors, including Richard Dreyfus, Gary Sinise, Jason Alexander, and Marisa Tomei. The app is easy to use, and you can follow along with the text right on the app. It is not free, but well worth the cost.

From a listening standpoint only, my favorite audio Bible is *The Bible Experience.* I access it through Audible these days (used to have it on my iPod) and while I love the actual product, it is hard to navigate if you are looking for individual books of the Bible. If you want to read straight through from beginning to end with an audio Bible, though, it costs just one Audible credit for members and is a compelling work by an all African American cast featuring Blair Underwood as Jesus and other prominent voices including Cuba Gooding Jr., Angela Bassett, and Denzel Washington.

Faith Comes By Hearing is a website that gives access to the spoken word of God in 1,843 languages as of August 2023, in 1,978 languages as of January 2024, and in 2,033 languages as of May 2024. How cool is that?! The goal of Faith Comes By Hearing is to "freely provide Scripture in every language that needs it by the year 2033, working to fulfill Jesus' Great Commission in this generation."

There are many options available to you for audio Bibles. I have friends who swear by Dwell and others who love YouVersion. Find one that works for you and don't feel guilty using it! It counts!

Learn to Rest in the Word

Do you ever find yourself reading with anxiety or performance in mind? Perhaps that is just me and my Type A tendencies. When I'm studying or prepping to teach, there are times that I slip into full-on academic mode and lock into the Word of God like work. I think there is some appropriateness to this since Paul exhorts Timothy to "Be diligent to present yourself approved to God as a workman who does not need to be ashamed, accurately handling the word of truth" (2 Timothy 2:15).

Good Bible study involves time, diligence, and some elbow grease—more on that in the next chapter—but the Word should also be our refuge, a place to simply commune with God and enjoy His presence. While I love study, I find the most enjoyment in God as I read His Word widely and rest in Him as I do.

But you might ask, "What if I find something earth-shattering as I'm reading? Am I supposed to just keep going and relaxing in the Word?" Well, you'll have to play that by ear. You may want to jot a quick note down in a margin and ask the Lord to help you continue to see how that truth will unfold and trust Him to do that.

Don't Be Ruled By Your Emotions

The earth won't move every time you read the Bible. Sometimes it will, but don't count on it every day. Some days God will seem so near that you'll hardly be able to comprehend it. Other days He'll seem distant. (It's not Him who's moved, by the way!) Just keep going. Keep putting the Word in and letting Him work on conforming you to look more and more like Jesus. Realize that the changes may be imperceptible to you at the start, but chances are that others around you will begin to notice something different and all of a sudden, you'll realize that things that used to be very important to you are not so much any more while things of eternal significance replace them.

Not allowing emotions to rule our thinking is especially important in reading widely. When we study deeply and plant in a specific portion of Scripture, we can run to places that resonate with us. Some of us love the gospels, others like to hang out in the Psalms. It can be easy to punt on a Bible read-through because Leviticus just isn't "doing it for me" and "I feel so much better when I read the Psalms." Hey, if you always want to read the Psalms, go ahead and add that to your wide reading, but don't run away from taking in the whole counsel of God's Word because of an emotional response or nonresponse.

Culture preaches that we should seek emotional payoff. We want goose bumps and a certain feeling in the pit of our stomach—we live in a world high on emotion, after all—but that is not what Christianity is about. It is about confidence and hope in God; it is about a sound mind and a clean heart and a life led by the indwelling Spirit of the living God that results in a deep and abiding joy, not tears and goose bumps coaxed out from low lights, high decibels, and well-timed fog machines.

Our culture tells us to trust in our hearts. The Bible teaches the opposite. Jeremiah writes that "The heart is deceitful above all things and desperately wicked . . ." (Jeremiah 17:9a). You can't trust your emotions. Like a toddler, sometimes they tell us the truth, but often they lie and, my oh my, can they be manipulative. Enjoy them when they're sober, but whatever you do, don't hand them the car keys.

GO WIDE STRATEGY

Watch for the Connections

As you're reading widely, you'll be seeing the through storyline of the text but you'll also be watching for connections. You'll begin to notice that the Bible begins and ends in a garden and has a garden in the middle at, arguably, the most climactic point of the whole Book. You'll see that God has always been a missionary God, saving some of the most unlikely people along the way. The genealogies that may bore you when you begin reading the Bible will become fascinating as you spend time and begin to meet the characters as their stories unfold. You'll notice the interesting ways that God leads people *out of* Egypt in a water event and *into* the Promised Land in another water event.

Remember the flyover of Alaska? You'll notice things differently when you're up close versus when you're high enough to take in a panorama. You'll see big things and little things. You'll start putting together pieces and figuring out that the famous Moabite Ruth of Ruth and Naomi fame had another mother-in-law, too, and when you realize who that is . . . your mind will be blown. Yeah, it will mean more to you when you discover it for yourself. Don't think for a minute that I'm spilling that spoiler!

GO WIDE STRATEGY

Follow Logical Progressions and Good Pairings

LOGICAL PROGRESSIONS AND GOOD PAIRINGS

As I'm reading widely, I tend to follow logical progressions. For example, I began my first read-through of the Bible with 1 and 2 Samuel followed by 1 and 2 Kings. I followed that up with the major prophet Jeremiah because I knew that at the end of Kings, the people go off into Babylonian captivity and Jeremiah is the prophet who is prophesying around the same time; Daniel and Ezekiel also prophesy during the same general time frame.

A New Testament example of this would be to read Luke followed by Acts. Luke wrote both accounts, so Acts is essentially the sequel to Luke's Gospel. Here are a few other progressions and pairings that you might find helpful.

67

LEVITICUS AND HEBREWS

I had a great childhood, for the most part. I knew without a doubt that my parents loved me, but . . . they made me eat vegetables. To this day, I can remember the taste and feel of cold beets, feel the squish of room-temp green beans, and vividly recall the gagging sensation as I tried to swallow each of them as close to whole as possible with a swig of warming milk. Every day my Dad would say, "Pam, if you'll just eat them while they're warm, and get it over with, it won't be so bad." And every day, I would dawdle at the dinner table until the veggies nearly molded on my plate.

All this to say that for me, reading through Leviticus a chapter a day is akin to my nightly vegetable marathon. An entire book of dos and don'ts for ancient Israel (I saw that yawn!), Leviticus pummels many would-be read-through-the-Bible types. Are there lessons to be learned in Leviticus? Absolutely! Will I see these lessons the first time I read through it? Maybe not. Will it be as fun or fulfilling to read as the Gospel of John? No. Still, regardless of what you seem to "get out of it" the first time through, even Leviticus will help you understand the whole context of the Bible. It will help you see how high and extensive the standards of God are and how impossible it is to be a law-keeper. It will help you to understand the seriousness of sin and the holiness of God.

Is Leviticus a place to stop and study deeply? Eventually. On a first trip through the Bible, though, I'd suggest pairing it with Hebrews to see the rigor of the old covenant held up against the grace of the new!

For those who are soldiering through the Bible from front to back, Leviticus presents itself early in the journey. It is not an easy read, but pairing it with the New Testament book of Hebrews can make all the difference in the world.

I know I'm probably not supposed to have favorites among biblical books, but historically Leviticus has been a bottom-3 book for me while Hebrews is easily a top-3 on my favorites list. Pairing Leviticus and

HEBREWS | LEVITICUS

When reading Leviticus mixing in passages from Hebrews
will bring context and new life to your reading.

☐ Leviticus 1–6

☐ Hebrews 1–4

☐ Leviticus 7–10

☐ Hebrews 5–7

☐ Leviticus 11–17

☐ Hebrews 8–10

☐ Leviticus 18–24

☐ Hebrews 11–12

☐ Leviticus 25–27

☐ Hebrews 13

Hebrews helps me to appreciate Leviticus in new ways and to love the book of Hebrews even more!

1 AND 2 KINGS AND MATTHEW

If you're tired of feeling in the dark when reading genealogies, do a quick read of 1 and 2 Kings and head directly to the Gospel of Matthew. Oh yeah. All of a sudden those distant names will be familiar! Although not every genealogy in Scripture will open up with cross-references like Matthew will, the first time you start recognizing many names in a genealogy is a huge payoff.

JONAH AND NAHUM

You probably know the story of Jonah. Did you know the rest of the story about Nineveh? If not, you'll find it in Nahum. Remember that the minor prophet who recounts Nineveh's story also starts with the letter "N." It's how I remember the connection!

DANIEL, ESTHER, NEHEMIAH, EZRA

Although Daniel sits with the prophets in your Bible, the books of Daniel, Esther, Nehemiah, and Ezra all follow the people of Judah after God's judgment falls on them at the hands of Babylon in 586 BC. Daniel records time in Babylonian captivity and the subsequent fall of Babylon, while Esther, Nehemiah, and Ezra tell of God's people in the aftermath, with some returning to the land of Judah to rebuild the temple and the wall of Jerusalem.

THE PSALMS ALONGSIDE OF 1 AND 2 SAMUEL

Since much of the book of Psalms is attributed to David, reading them alongside of the narratives about him in 1 and 2 Samuel works well.

GO WIDE STRATEGY
Intermix the Easy with the More Difficult

Sometimes you'll find a logical path to the next book. Other times you'll need the pragmatism of simply finding an easy win or hitting a single. When I'm having a hard time reading—it happens to everyone at times—I hit singles. I find short books to build momentum instead of trying to grit my teeth and grind through Ezekiel. Yes, sometimes I also give myself prizes. More on that later. :)

Remember that the Old Testament Is Filled with Stories

Indulge me here for one more quick point on the Old Testament. Have you picked up a children's Bible anytime recently? If so, what have you seen? That's right, you've seen stories from the Old Testament, and lots of them. Sure, you'll find accounts about Jesus, too, and a few about Paul, but you'll have tons of Old Testament stories. I don't use the word "story" here in the sense of something fictitious or mythological as some might, but to help you connect with the truth that much of the Old Testament captivates even children! When brought to the appropriate developmental level, it holds the attention of even the toughest audiences. It's also understandable to kids, which means you can understand it, too!

Get In and Trust God

Get off the fence and get moving if you are an I-have-to-understand-everything type of a person. It's incredibly easy to talk yourself out of reading widely if you think you have to understand everything right away. If you are truly a child of God and seek Him through His Word, God will use that Word to affect radical change in your life. Again, God will use the Word in your life. You obey by seeking Him while trusting that only He can change you, only He can give you understanding. That being the case, your job, my job is to abide in the Vine (John 15), to put the Word in and allow the Lord to do the work in us. Overthinking when you're reading widely can stop you cold. When your overthinker weighs in, remind that part of your brain that you will find more of the answers as you study deeply and as you continue to read and discover more in the extended context.

71

Don't Fall for the Lie of Being a "New Testament Only" Christian

If you've been a Christian for a while and have never read the Old Testament, you may have reasoned to yourself that because we have a new covenant in Jesus Christ, we don't need to read about the old covenant. As rationalizations go, it sounds pretty good. Given a choice between the two, certainly you'd have to go with the New Testament. Where this breaks down, though, is that you will never grasp the wonder of the new covenant without first understanding the gravity of the old. Much of the New Testament will remain a closed book to you because you won't understand the foundation and you won't have a full understanding of God.

I run into students all the time who become frustrated reading and studying the New Testament, because they don't know or understand the Old Testament foundation. God gave us the entire Bible for a reason; we need to be about the business of reading all of it.

Not only that, the New Testament tells us that the Old Testament provides us examples, both good and bad, about how we should (or should not!) live. In 1 Corinthians 10:6, the apostle Paul writes to the church at Corinth about the wilderness generation of Israelites, saying, "Now these things happened as examples for us, so that we would not crave evil things as they also craved."

The Israelites showed themselves to be idolators who acted immorally, grumbled, and brought judgment on themselves. Paul goes on to write, in verses 11-12, "Now these things happened to them as an example, and they were written for our instruction, upon whom the ends of the ages have come. Therefore let him who thinks he stands take heed that he does not fall." Honestly, the lessons I've learned on grumbling alone from the Old Testament have been worth the price of admission!

GO WIDE STRATEGY
Would You Have the Time for $1,000?

We all have twenty-four hours in a day. Thus, to say that you simply do not have time to read through the Bible when others can find the time comes down to a matter of priority. We all know this. Sure, some have fewer responsibilities than others, but we all have the choice of our priorities. We all have twenty-four hours to steward and spend.

Let's think about this together. Say I offered you $1,000 cash—or Venmo if you prefer—if you would read just ten pages of your Bible today. Could you find the time to do that? That's $100 per page. What do you think? In over 30 years of teaching I've only had one person look me in the eyes and say, "I would not have the time." I'm guessing that person could make an excuse for anything. Let's say that you accept my gracious offer. I show up at your doorstep tomorrow and hand you ten crisp $100 bills for having read ten pages of the Bible.

Let's say that I offer to show up at your house every single day at 1:00 p.m. and give you $1,000 every day that you read ten pages of the Bible. Could you figure it out?

I trust you see my point. We make time for whatever we truly value and choose to make time for. To say that you "just don't have the time" to read your Bible widely and to invest in the Word of God means you are too busy. Plain and simple. You choose how you spend your time. Do it wisely.

You've been reading awhile! How about you put this book down for a bit and get into The Book. Pick a strategy or two and see how it goes. When you need a bit more encouragement, come on back and we'll look at some more wide reading strategies in the next chapter.

DRAW NEAR THIS WEEK

Pick one or more of these opportunities for drawing near. Remember to pray before you start reading that God will teach you through His Word!

- Start or continue reading the Gospel of John to help you begin building the habit of daily fixing your eyes on Jesus.
- Start reading in 1 Samuel if you're already a pro in Genesis. Remember to put your pencil down and try to read in increments of at least 30 minutes as you're building your reading habit.
- Start reading in Genesis if you've never read it before. If you can, see if you can read in increments of at least 30 minutes.

DISCUSS TOGETHER

These questions can be used in a discussion group if you're using this book in a Bible study setting or book club. You can also use them to process through what you're learning on your own.

- Where have you been reading in the Word this week?
  - How has it been going?
- What translation of the Bible have you selected?
  - Why did you choose it?
  - Are you pleased with your selection?
- Were you able to identify any specific lies that you've believed with regard to your Bible reading?
  - What truths are you using to combat lies you've identified?
- What new strategies have you been trying this week?
  - What has worked?
  - What strategies are you thinking about trying this week?
- How have you felt about putting the pencil down?
  - Has it been freeing or difficult for you?
- Have you tried an audio Bible this week or previously?
  - If so, which one and how did it go?
  - If not, is there a reason why?
- Were you able to make some time for "chunk" reading this week?
  - If so, how did it go?
- Do you feel like you're making progress? Explain.
- What concerns do you need to bring to the Lord?

READ TOGETHER

If you're meeting with a group, spend some of your time reading the Bible aloud. Take turns with each person reading several verses up to a chapter, depending on the size of your group. Again, if you have a larger group, break up into smaller groups of no more than five people each, and don't pressure anyone into reading who isn't comfortable reading aloud.

This week read Paul's letter to the **Galatians**. It should take you about 20 minutes. In Galatians you'll learn some of the backstory of the Apostle Paul who wrote more books than any other New Testament author and you'll hear a clear exposition of the gospel.

When you're finished, pray for one another that God will continue to draw you near to Him through His Word.

CHAPTER 4

More Strategies for Reading Wide

Plus Some Practical Help With History!

READING WIDELY PAYS CUMULATIVE DIVIDENDS like interest on an investment. As you read widely, you not only learn individual truths, but you see how God's truth through Scripture fits together in such a way that you end up with more than the sum of the parts. It often takes some time before we start seeing connections for ourselves, but when we do, there is nothing like it! Truth you discover for yourself as you engage with the Word of God is so much sweeter than truth that you pick up secondhand from someone else's work.

That said, we all benefit from some general guidelines and structure to equip us to study for ourselves. So before we jump into more practical tips and strategies for reading widely, let's take a quick moment for a sidebar history lesson that will help give you a solid start as you navigate the Old Testament historical books in particular.

SIDEBAR HISTORY LESSON

The Old Testament tells us, among other things, about the history of the people of Israel. Along the way, however, we start seeing other names associated with God's people. Judah emerges, as well as references to Jerusalem and Samaria. At first glance, the names can be quite confusing, but Old Testament history is easier than you'd first think once you lock into a few simple, orienting facts.

FAMILY TREE

The people of Israel take their name from the grandson of Abraham, whom we hear referenced as Jacob in the early chapters of Genesis. God, however, renames him Israel, and from this comes the name of the Jewish people as a whole—Israel. You might be wondering why people from Israel are today referred to as Jews. Good question! More on that in a moment.

DEFINITIONS

ISRAEL —The name given to Jacob by God means *struggles* or *wrestles with God*. It's an upgrade from Jacob which meant *supplanter* or *heel-grabber*. *Israel* later becomes the name of the nation descended from him. During the time of the monarchy, Israel becomes a divided nation with two of the twelve tribes remaining with Rehoboam, the son of Solomon, while the other ten tribes follow Jeroboam. These ten tribes retain the name Israel. The capital of Israel was Samaria. It is also referred to as the *Northern Kingdom*. All of the kings of the North were evil, some more and some less. Israel was captured in 722 BC by Assyria. Most of the inhabitants were deported and scattered; the remaining ones intermarried with other people groups who were brought into Israel by Assyria. In this way, the Assyrians controlled conquered nations.

JUDAH — Judah, the man, was one of the sons of Jacob (Israel) who became the father of one of the twelve tribes of Israel. It was from the tribe of Judah that the Davidic kings descended and the tribe from which Messiah would come. After the division of the kingdom, however, Judah also came to refer to the two tribes that remained with Rehoboam, the son of Solomon, while the other ten tribes followed Jeroboam and were referred to as Israel. The capital of Judah was Jerusalem. It is also referred to as the *Southern Kingdom*. In the Southern Kingdom, the kings were a mixed bag: some were good, some bad, and others terrible! Jerusalem, the capital city of Judah, fell to the Babylonians in 586 BC. Babylon carted off the inhabitants into a 70-year captivity—prophesied by Jeremiah—after which they were allowed to return to the land. The term *Jewish* originates from Judah. While the ten tribes of Israel were scattered, Judah returned from captivity. Hence the terms *Jew* and *Jewish*. To summarize:

- Judah was a man
- Judah was the tribe descended from him
- Judah is also referred to as the Southern Kingdom made up of the tribes of Judah and Benjamin

EPHRAIM —While the Northern Kingdom is usually referred to as Israel, it is occasionally called Ephraim. This is not a veiled attempt to confuse you, although I'd understand if you thought it might be! Ephraim—one of Joseph's sons, and the tribe of Moses' successor Joshua—was the largest tribe in the Northern Kingdom. Because of this, it is sometimes used to refer to the Northern Kingdom as a whole.

SAMARIA — Samaria was the capital of Israel, the Northern Kingdom of ten tribes that followed non-Davidic kings.

JERUSALEM —— Jerusalem was the capital of Judah, the Southern Kingdom. Again, the Southern Kingdom was comprised primarily of the tribes of Judah and Benjamin (plus many of the Levites), and the kings came from the Davidic line.

UNITED KINGDOM —— Israel was a United Kingdom of twelve tribes under the leadership first of Saul, and then of David and his son, Solomon.

DIVIDED KINGDOM —— Because Solomon's heart turned from the Lord to follow other gods, God took ten tribes away during the reign of his son Rehoboam. Rehoboam for his part followed the unwise advice of his cronies which prompted the ten tribes to follow after Jeroboam, a servant of Solomon's who became king in the north.

NORTHERN KINGDOM —— Ten northern tribes ruled by non-Davidic kings. Also referred to as *Israel*. The capital was Samaria.

SOUTHERN KINGDOM —— Two southern tribes ruled by the Davidic line of kings and comprised of the tribes of Judah and Benjamin, plus many of the Levites. Some from other tribes who continued to follow God also migrated to the Southern Kingdom as well. The Southern Kingdom is referred to simply as *Judah*. The capital, established by King David, was Jerusalem.

While this may seem like too much information, please consider it a resource particularly as you read the historical and prophetic books to help keep the players straight. Now let's get back to some more tips and strategies for reading wide.

MORE TIPS AND STRATEGIES FOR READING WIDE

Remember to use the tips that work for you in your situation. Feel free to skip over entries that don't apply, but lean into those that encourage, convict, or inspire.

GO WIDE STRATEGY
Remember to Keep Praying

Pray for the desire to read. Pray before you read. Pray as you read! You know this already. I know this already. If you're like me, you probably need to be reminded. You are not alone on this journey; continue to ask God to lead the way!

GO WIDE STRATEGY
Use Mind Games to Your Benefit

Success tends to breed more success, and failure usually breeds continued failure. Discipline breeds discipline, indulgence breeds indulgence. We all know this from just living our lives and watching the lives of others. Take school, for example. Scoring well on a test tends to buoy up a student and spur him or her on to greater things. Score 98% on a test, you know you've got the right stuff and can pull it off again; land a 40% after having exerted yourself and it is much harder to gain the courage to try again.

Let's face it: even for people who succeed in other areas of life, reading through the Bible often proves difficult so it's important to foster even the small successes that build momentum. Think with me for a moment about the typical path most people take in reading the Bible, bearing in mind that when you look at the Bible's table of contents you're staring at a list of sixty-six entries. If you start in Genesis and proceed forward, you have ninety chapters in just your first two books. While these books are engaging reading (respectfully excluding the final twenty chapters of Exodus), the checkmarks for "books read" in your table of contents aren't exactly flying onto the page.

So by the time you hit the Leviticus/Numbers wall, you don't have much in the way of visual success to look at in your table of contents. If you've read Genesis and Exodus, you have covered a great deal of ground—truly, you have done well!—but you will likely feel less on a roll than if you had knocked off a few of the shorter books first. A "spiritual" way of doing things? Maybe not, but it has worked for me. I've found that as I do what I can to get God's Word into my life, He has a way of being faithful and doing the spiritual work in me from the inside out.

GO WIDE STRATEGY

Read Epistles in Their Entirety

Who reads letters in segments? Um, no one. An epistle is a letter—even the lengthier Romans, Hebrews, and 1 Corinthians are letters. How do you read a letter? Most of us read a letter in one sitting. You don't say, "Okay, I'll read three paragraphs today, three tomorrow, and three on Friday," do you? Of course not. We read a letter as a whole. That's the way to do the epistles, too, especially as you're reading the Word widely.

For as long as I can remember, five-minute devotionals have been standard fare among many American evangelicals. With the rise of the internet and the steady decline of the adult attention span, we have more and more people who no longer know how to sit down, focus, and digest a larger portion of Scripture; how to interact and read for more than ten or fifteen minutes at a time. Reading New Testament letters in one sitting is a way to turn the tide.

GO WIDE STRATEGY

Read History Before Prophecy

If you don't understand some of the history of Israel, the prophets will be unduly difficult. So, while you don't want to shelve the prophets for too long, you also don't want to start with them. Before you jump into the prophets, get yourself through 1 and 2 Samuel and 1 and 2 Kings.

Those four books will give you a decent base for your first dip into the prophets. Even if you add Deuteronomy, the prophets will still take some work. Don't fret when you see things you don't understand. Chalk the experience up to context and keep reading. Remember, reading the Bible is not a one-and-done event. We learn over a lifetime!

Read Minor Prophets in Their Entirety

As with the epistles, you're better off reading the minor prophets in one sitting. Each of these books is relatively short, hence the term "minor." They are not less important than Isaiah, Jeremiah, and Ezekiel, but they're much quicker reads. The minor prophets are Hosea, Joel, Amos, Obadiah, Jonah, Micah, Nahum, Habakkuk, Zephaniah, Haggai, Zechariah, and Malachi. The books range in length from one chapter to fourteen. When reading the prophets, it is essential that you ask at the

If you don't have a basic understanding of the history of Israel and the concept of covenant, you'll do well to read Deuteronomy and some of the historical books—Joshua, Judges, 1 and 2 Kings—before moving into the prophets.

very least, these two basic question to gain a simple understanding of the book:

1. Who is the prophecy written to? The answer will usually be Israel (the Northern Kingdom), Judah (the Southern Kingdom), or both. Occasionally, prophesies address other nations in Israel's orbit.

2. When was it written?

The answer you are looking for is either *before* or *after* the nation has been conquered. Has the nation already been conquered due to judgment, or is the book looking ahead to and predicting coming judgment?

Again, if you don't have a basic understanding of the history of Israel and the concept of covenant, you'll do well to read Deuteronomy and some of the historical books—Joshua, Judges, 1 and 2 Samuel, 1 and 2 Kings—before moving into the prophets. If, however, you have the basic gist of the divided kingdom and the subsequent captivities, feel free to zip through the minor prophets early on and finish what looks in the table of contents to be about a quarter of the Old Testament. Remember to use the Sidebar History Lesson earlier in this chapter as a reference as you wade into the deeper waters.

When Reading Is Hard

I could tell you that once you start reading the Bible consistently it will become easy and you will never struggle. I could tell you that, but I would be lying. Regularly reading the Bible will make it easier and as you walk with the Spirit in the Word, there will be joy, but you will still encounter difficult times along the way. I think everyone does; at least I do.

Sometimes reading the Bible feels too hard. Maybe you're behind at work or the kids are being unbearable. Maybe you have a Great Dane and you're babysitting two Corgis and the three decide to perform *a cappella* for every passing delivery truck and neighbor. Perhaps you've been burning the candle at both ends so long that all you can do is doom scroll on your phone or watch YouTube videos. Whether it's spiritual warfare or just the circumstances of life, there will be times when opening your Bible is tough. That's when it's the most important to "just do it." Don't dive into martyr mode, though. You know what I mean, right? "Oh, I know that I should read my Bible, so I'll just sit here and read Leviticus since I'm already feeling miserable and let's see how I can apply *that* in my life today!"

If you're struggling, go for the low-hanging fruit and park in the easier books for a bit. I find the historical books and the gospels—any of Matthew, Mark, Luke, or John—to be the easiest to read because I love

84

stories, as most people do. Others find the Psalms or Proverbs easier to read when they're in a stuck place.

Let's Talk Major Prophets

Hit the major prophets (Isaiah, Jeremiah, Ezekiel), Leviticus, and Numbers when you have established momentum, but make sure you knock off at least one major prophet relatively early in your reading so you're not "looking forward" to all of them all year long.

Some of you may have been stopped by the fact that I didn't include Daniel when I referred to the major prophets. While Daniel is usually lumped in with this group, it is much shorter and immanently more readable. You could easily park yourself and polish it off in one enjoyable sitting, even without a latte at your side. In fact, the time it takes to read Daniel from start to finish is less than a typical Sunday morning church service.

The big three, on the other hand, are all in the fifty-chapter range, and although they are God's true and living Word, the prophets tend to be tougher to grasp on a first trip through the Bible than some of the other biblical texts. They're tougher on second and third trips, too, but each repetition brings them into clearer focus. So while you will find treasures in the major prophets even without much background (for example, Isaiah 53, the descriptions of God in Ezekiel, etc.) some of the material will leave you scratching your head . . . and that's okay . . . for now. Remember, the first time you're reading through the Bible, you're looking for the big picture, the broad strokes, the context of how it all fits together. Details are important, but many of them will come later.

Whatever you do, don't be afraid of the prophets to the point that you avoid them. When you're ready, jump in and start to swim. I remember being fascinated the first time I read Jeremiah. Did I understand it all? Not even close. But I was struck by the characterization of the people of Judah and their stiff-necked manner and unrepentant hearts, and I came to a better understanding of why God was disciplining them. It wasn't for one bad choice. It was for bad choice after bad choice after bad choice. After my "indignant" phase with them, I also realized how much like them I often tend to be . . . and I have the benefit of the indwelling Holy Spirit, which they did not have. Ouch. Let's just say that even though I didn't understand everything, what I did understand did its work in such a way that it is still memorable to me 35+ years later.

The more you understand the historical books and the books of the Law, the more the prophets will open up. These books will give you plenty to work on for years. Don't be discouraged by that; be encouraged that you'll never run out!

Identify Encumbrances

Wide reading takes time, but there is no better investment you can make. As I mentioned, getting serious with God involved some decision-making for me. We all have 24 hours in a day, but it is easy to fritter them away without realizing where the time is going. Getting rid of *Sports Illustrated* and *The Sun Times* was not pleasant in the moment, but it was a small sacrifice that made a huge difference in my life.

Along the way, we also cut the cable in our home. I know, you're laughing now, right? Cutting the cable worked for awhile, but then came Netflix and Hulu and YouTube. Encumbrances, like COVID, produce variants and the internet is the king of all variants shifting to allure us in new ways every single day.

A key way that I watch my time is with a simple time tracker called Toggl. Because my workday involves working for the King and stewarding kingdom resources, it is critical for me to know that I am investing my time wisely. I use Toggl to track how I spend my time. Right now I'm using it to see how many words I can write in an hour. If you're having trouble finding time in the day to be in the Word, download Toggl or a similar app and simply track what you do with your time for a few days.

Your issue won't be the now defunct *Sports Illustrated,* but I'll bet that time tracking will surface some time suckers in your life.

Don't Drown in the Details

Pay attention to the details (genealogies, etc.) as you read widely, but don't allow yourself to be bogged down by them now.

If you have to skim a bit on genealogies, Levitical laws, the beginning of the book of Numbers or the end of Ezekiel with its detailed measurements of the future temple, don't flog yourself over it. Genealogies did nothing but annoy me the first couple of times I read through the Bible. You may feel the same way. Most people do. If you put in the time over some years, though, you'll find that genealogies will morph along the way. This is one of the surprising payoffs that you'll discover after you've put in the time in God's Word. Facts and sections that once seemed boring, trivial, or irrelevant will start to come into focus as you begin to meet more and more of the characters and as you start to understand the whole.

Take Rahab, for instance. You've probably noticed Rahab in the line of Jesus. That may seem unremarkable to you unless you've read her story in the book of Joshua, or perhaps you've read both and have become immune to the wonder of it. She is the one person in the city of Jericho who not only believes that the God of the Israelites is powerful, but also that He might save *her* if she asks! She's a name in a genealogy in Matthew, but when we hear her whole story, we find out that she is not only a woman of ill-repute, but also a flat out foreigner in a city destined for destruction.

As we read more we begin to see connections. We come to know many of the people mentioned in the genealogies and the Scriptures continue to unfold more and more to us.

GO WIDE STRATEGY
Seriously, Don't Get Bogged Down When Reading Wide

If you happen to be a perfectionist, I know that you've already discounted what I've said about allowing yourself to speed up and even skim a little in the difficult parts of the Old Testament. You may be thinking, I want to see the connections now! I, too, struggle with perfectionism and I know that you're thinking, "Hey, if you haven't really read everything, you haven't read everything." My advice (to you and me!): loosen up. I know, I know, easier said than done, but just for fun give it a whirl. If you feel that guilty (some of our church backgrounds bend us this way), next time through you can memorize the genealogies. ;)

GO WIDE STRATEGY
Relax and Enjoy!

Enjoy the Word! Be diligent, yes. But don't be uptight. Don't set the clock; don't get the guilts and try to make it up when you miss a day. Find a comfortable spot to sit, put your feet up, and learn to enjoy spending time with your God. View your time in His Word as a time of rest and restoration. If reading through the Bible in a year is too fast for you, then find a comfortable pace and lean into that.

GO WIDE STRATEGY
Reframe Reading as a "Get To Do" Instead of a "Got To Do"

When my kids were in elementary school, the number of parents at class parties were limited to four per event. The only way to attend all of the class parties was to be the Head Room Mom, aka the Big Kahuna. My first year as the Big Kahuna was wildly stressful for me since I was still learning what did and did not work with grade school children—and since I am just better with high school age and up. I'll never forget on one particularly busy day prior to the politically correct "Holiday Party," all of the last-minute stuff seemed like such a burden. I'm not a craft lady. I'm not much in the kitchen. I just wanted to help with my kid's party.

I was well on the road to a cranky day when I realized: "I don't *have* to do this. I *get* to do this." My paradigm shifted dramatically. I had an opportunity! How many others wanted to do what I was getting to do but couldn't because of work commitments or other encumbrances? How fortunate I was to have this fun opportunity with my son and his classmates! How fortunate you and I are to have a Bible of our own and the chance to meet with God whenever we want to without fear of persecution!

GO WIDE STRATEGY
Don't Just Plan . . . Do It!

I like planning things to do, but sometimes the actual doing of them is tougher. Right now, you are preparing to start because you are reading this book. This will only be time well spent if you don't get stuck here. Don't spend your Bible-reading time making a schedule or reading commentaries about the Bible. Don't fritter away your time with footnotes or general inspirational literature. Read the Bible. Jump in and get started! Pray and move forward. Yes, commentaries are great (after you've studied!) and devotionals can help and encourage, but they need to be in addition to the Bible, not in place of it. They are not God-breathed. The Bible is!

GO WIDE STRATEGY
Ignore Chapter Breaks

The chapter and verse breaks in your Bible are not inspired. Helpful as they are in navigating the Bible, they hamper us when we're simply trying to read. They cause us to stop and start like a car in downtown Chicago. Learning to ignore the chapter breaks will cause your reading to be more like an uninterrupted ride through Utah! In addition, as you read you'll find several places where chapter and verse breaks actually detract from meaning by grouping content away from its natural context. This isn't typical, but it happens!

Feeling Behind? Hit Singles!

When you're feeling behind in your Bible reading for whatever reason, read several shorter books in a single sitting—minor prophets and epistles both fit the bill. I realize that this may sound unspiritual (again!), but God can change our hearts and minds through His Word even when we use pragmatic approaches. Sometimes we just need a mental boost of checking off a few books, and with twelve minor prophets ranging in length from one chapter (Obadiah) to fourteen (Hosea and Zechariah), the minor prophets are a place you can feel like you're making some quick progress. There are also four one-chapter epistles—Philemon, 2 and 3 John, and Jude. Hey, sometimes you just need a win!

Avoid Footnotes

Footnotes are well-meaning helps, but you need to avoid them as much as possible. They are one person's view of the text you are reading. If you don't understand something, go back and look at the context, don't jump to the footnotes. If you hang out in the footnotes, you'll be inadvertently buying into a theological school of thought rather than searching the Scriptures for yourself and allowing the Holy Spirit to be your teacher. Are they helpful? Sure. Sometimes. Same thing with commentaries. They can be valuable tools *after* you've done the digging for yourself.

Read Psalms and Proverbs Concurrently with Something Else

Chances are you'll love reading the Psalms and Proverbs, provided you don't try to read straight through. I suggest reading these concurrently with something else. Sure, you can read through five or six Psalms in one sitting and learn from them, for example, how to better worship. You can sit in a smaller number and let them work their way through you. If you try to reel off twenty or thirty at a time, though, you'll overdose. You won't appreciate the poetry, the worship, the depth of emotion if you read it in the same way as you read narrative portions of Scripture. Even when you're in read-wide mode, you'll want to slow down and meditate on the Psalms. Don't rush. Let them soak into your soul as you read. Pick a favorite, memorize it, let the Holy Spirit teach you how to worship through it.

At the same time, however, be aware that there are 150 Psalms. You can do the math. If you read one Psalm per day, it'll take you nearly half a year to make your way through this book. That's fine if you're also reading somewhere else at the same time and you happen to be a plodder. Sprinters (like me) will go crazy at a Psalm-a-day pace. Better for us to read five to ten a day and feel great about our "chapter volume" for a bit.

Long story, short: the Psalms are an outlier, a book that you'll need to experiment with a bit to find the best way for you to work through it. There is not a right way. The wrong way is, of course, avoidance. ;)

> *Long story, short: the Psalms are an outlier, a book that you'll need to experiment with a bit to find the best way for you to work through it.*

The Proverbs, on the other hand, will give you good guidelines for life; short, pithy sayings that generally prove true if carried out. Again, they are best taken in a chapter or two a day. Otherwise, due to the brevity of the sayings and the cyclical repetition of them throughout the book, they will run together into a wise-words stew with much wisdom but too much to think about in terms of action.

Another variant to the chapter or two a day option is to read through the Proverbs more quickly watching for specific topics. Take the mouth, for instance. You may want to read straight through the Proverbs in one or two sittings and mark everything you learn about how you use your tongue, but that may be way too actionable! Just saying.

One of the bigger mistakes people tend to make when reading the Proverbs is believing they are actual promises of God to them. They simply are not. Yes, the Bible does contain many promises; they just are not found in the book of Proverbs. Proverbs are life principles, which generally hold true. Important? Yes. Helpful? Absolutely. Don't start doubting or accusing God when you see outliers to the general principles in the book.

By the way, there are thirty-one chapters in the book of Proverbs. That makes it a great one-chapter-a-day read to pair with just about anything else you're reading in the Word.

GO WIDE STRATEGY

Remember It's Not a One-and-Done Event

As you read widely remind yourself that reading through the Bible will not be a one-time, bucket-list event. Honestly, the minute you determine to continue reading the Word, the pressure for immediate and total understanding vanishes. Sure, if you're that "type" (and I speak as one who is), having some questions will eventually spur you on to more study, and that's great. That's what should happen; that's part of the approach of going both deep and wide in Scripture. The point here is to keep the questions you have in your wide reading from derailing you as you seek to gain enough context for deep study. You're not ignoring questions, you're taking the first step toward answering them by gaining the additional information that context and extended context provide.

I love how much context the Bible provides! First, it provides the context of the book in which the material appears, and beyond that, the context of the whole Bible. Since Scripture interprets Scripture, you'll find that the difficult passages in certain areas will clear up dramatically when you read other parts of Scripture, but you have to be reading the whole Word of God for this principle to work.

GO WIDE STRATEGY

Learn to Be an Active Reader

While we're not trying to answer every question the first time through the Word of God, that doesn't preclude interacting vigorously with the text and asking questions as you read. "Who is writing? Why is he writing? Who are the intended recipients?" In order to catch what is going on, we need to train ourselves to ask questions of the text in the course of our reading to help us see the whole picture. Think back to the journalistic five Ws and H to help you as you read:

- Who is writing? Who is it written to?
- What is the point? What is the writer trying to get across to his readers?
- Where is the book written from? Where is the audience located? Where are the locations mentioned?
- Why did the author write?
- When was the book written?
- Are there any specific "How?" questions that the text answers?

Eventually, you'll answer these questions in writing if you're studying the text deeply, but for now as you're reading answer them in your head as you go along. Be like a journalist of old—ask questions, get answers!

Watch How God Makes Himself Known

When I read widely, there is one phrase that I mark consistently. Whenever I see references to God acting in such a way that people will "know" Him, I mark the text. Here are a couple of examples (note that the boldface is mine):

Exodus 10:1-2

1   Then the LORD said to Moses, "Go to Pharaoh, for I have hardened his heart and the heart of his servants, that I may perform these signs of Mine among them,

2   and that you may tell in the hearing of your son, and of your grandson, how I made a mockery of the Egyptians and how I performed My signs among them, **that you may know that I am the LORD.**"

Ezekiel 12:16

16   "But I will spare a few of them from the sword, the famine and the pestilence that they may tell all their abominations among the nations where they go, and **may know that I am the LORD.**"

Watch How Everything Points to Jesus

This will take some time, but as you continue to read the Bible, you will see more and more the way everything points to Jesus. Watch particularly how the New Testament authors quote the Old Testament to start seeing the connections. I could give you a list, but what fun would that be? The Old Testament points to Jesus over and over again . . . watch for it!

DRAW NEAR THIS WEEK

Pick one or more of the opportunities for drawing near. Some of the options this week are the same as last week, so feel free to continue with what you have been reading if you are in the middle of John, 1 Samuel, or Genesis.

- Start or continue reading the Gospel of John to help you begin building the habit of daily fixing your eyes on Jesus.
- Start reading in 1 Samuel if you're already a pro in Genesis. Remember to put your pencil down and try to read in increments of at least 30 minutes as you're building your reading habit.
- Start reading in Genesis if you've never read it before. If you can, see if you can read in increments of at least 30 minutes.
- Pick one or two of the following shorter epistles to read in one sitting: Galatians, Ephesians, Philippians, or Colossians.

DISCUSS TOGETHER

These questions can be used in a discussion group if you're using this book in a Bible study setting or book club. You can also use them to process through what you're learning on your own.

- Where have you been reading in the Word this week?
  - How has it been going?
  - What have been your biggest takeaways?
  - What questions have you had that may need further study?
- What new strategies have you been trying this week?
  - What has worked?
  - What strategies are you thinking about trying this week?
- How have your Bible reading habits been changing over the past few weeks?
  - Is reading becoming easier for you?
- Are you viewing your reading as a "get to do" or a "got to do"?
  - Has this changed?
- What are your biggest remaining struggles or frustrations?
  - Do you have strategies to confront these, or do you need additional tools?
- What concerns do you need to bring to the Lord?

READ TOGETHER

If you're meeting with a group, spend some of your time reading the Bible aloud. As always, those who prefer to listen can choose that as an option. This week take turns reading several verses each of the following historical summary chapters: **Psalm 105–106, Joshua 24, Acts 7, Acts 26,** and **Hebrews 11**. Each of these passages recounts and summarizes different portions of Israel's history. I think of them as "catch up" episodes. When you're finished reading, pray for one another that God will continue to draw you near to Him through His Word and that you will know Him better and better as a result.

CHAPTER 5

The Why and How of Going Deep

Simple Steps for Deep Study

WHATEVER HAPPENED TO THE SIMPLE CHEESEBURGER and fries? I love Chipotle as much as the next person, but the endless stream of questions involved in ordering a soft-shelled taco is sometimes more than I can bear. I'm grateful that my husband does most of our grocery shopping, because the sheer volume of choices there are even more overwhelming. *Consumer Reports* magazine stated back in 2014 that the average supermarket shelves 40,000 choices for its customers (more than four times that of supermarkets in the 1970s), and that Super WalMart locations offer a mind-boggling 100,000 items.

In response to the paralyzing choices, we are also seeing a rise in curated information and products. One of the best examples in the food arena is ALDI, a no-frills grocery store chain that stocks about 1,400 carefully selected items; ALDI is growing faster than any other grocery chain in the United States as of 2024.

Take media as another example. Netflix offers over 6,500 titles, Hulu over 7,000, and Amazon Prime an eye-popping 29,000 combined movie and television titles. With numbers that high, we rely more and more on curated information to make choices. There's no way to find our way without outside help.

Google curates information, as does Facebook, and every other app you interact with that runs on algorithms. They watch you and they deliver content designed especially for you.

Curated information helps us navigate an increasingly complex world. In most areas of my life, I'm all for it. When it comes to the Bible, however, I draw a line, because easier always comes with strings attached. With the Bible, we need to not only read widely, but also to study deeply so we will know God's truth for ourselves instead of relying on questionable curators and middlemen.

THE CHALLENGE OF STUDYING DEEPLY

The objection to deep Bible study that I hear most often is that it is just too hard. I love Kay Arthur's response to that objection with regard to inductive Bible study in particular. She always reminds people that inductive Bible study is not hard, it just takes time. She is right.

Perhaps the great challenge to deep Bible study today is not the difficulty of the material but the busyness of our schedules. Going deep in God's Word takes time. Learning to slow down may be the hardest part of the process for you.

While our e-world tempts us with distractions, it also provides us with unparalleled tools for accessing and studying God's Word. When I took Greek back in the days just after Plato had passed, we parsed verbs based on our knowledge of Greek grammar. Today anyone with computer access can parse verbs with the click of a mouse. There has never been an easier on-ramp to studying deeply than we have today!

WHY STUDY DEEPLY?

In a day and age when culture has deemed truth relative, here are just a few reasons to embrace deep study of God's Word.

1. STUDY DEEPLY BECAUSE TRUTH HAS STUMBLED IN THE STREETS.

Writing to the people of Judah in the eighth century BC, Isaiah describes a time and people with striking similarities to our culture today. Note in the following passages what he says about good, evil, light, darkness, and truth.

Isaiah 5:20-23

20 *Woe to those who call evil good, and good evil;*
Who substitute darkness for light and light for darkness;
Who substitute bitter for sweet and sweet for bitter!

21 *Woe to those who are wise in their own eyes*
And clever in their own sight!

22 *Woe to those who are heroes in drinking wine*
And valiant men in mixing strong drink,

23 *Who justify the wicked for a bribe,*
And take away the rights of the ones who are in the right!

Isaiah 59:14-15

14 *Justice is turned back,*
And righteousness stands far away;
For truth has stumbled in the street,
And uprightness cannot enter.

15 *Yes, truth is lacking;*
And he who turns aside from evil makes himself a prey.
Now the LORD saw,
And it was displeasing in His sight that there was no justice.

Like Judah in the days of Isaiah, we live in a world that often legislates wrong and punishes right. Although the United States was built on the Judeo-Christian ethic, that foundation is under attack and crumbling. We cannot look to culture for right and wrong, because truth has stumbled and justice is turned back. If you do not know for yourself from God's

Word that there is good and evil, right and wrong, culture's madness will eventually sweep you away. The world lies in the hands of the evil one (1 John 5:19) who is the father of lies (John 8:44). The way to stand is by knowing Truth!

2. STUDY DEEPLY TO ACCURATELY HANDLE GOD'S WORD.

In writing to Timothy just prior to his own death at the hands of Rome, Paul emphasizes the importance of diligent study of Scripture. Disciples are to handle the Word accurately so they can present themselves as approved workmen to God (2 Timothy 2:15). Scripture, Paul reminds Timothy, is inspired and equips the people of God thoroughly for every good work (2 Timothy 3:16).

The Bereans were an example of first century people doing just this. Luke tells us about them in Acts 17:10-12 when he writes of Paul and Silas visiting their city.

> ### Acts 17:10-12
> 10 *The brethren immediately sent Paul and Silas away by night to Berea, and when they arrived, they went into the synagogue of the Jews.*
> 11 *Now these were more noble-minded than those in Thessalonica, for they received the word with great eagerness, examining the Scriptures daily to see whether these things were so.*
> 12 *Therefore many of them believed, along with a number of prominent Greek women and men.*

3. STUDY DEEPLY BECAUSE YOU CAN'T LIVE WHAT YOU DON'T KNOW.

Peter tells us that through true knowledge of God we have everything needed for life and godliness (2 Peter 1:3). This is a tremendous assurance, but the fact remains that we cannot live what we do not know.

4. STUDY DEEPLY SO YOU DON'T HAVE TO RELY ON CURATED "TRUTH."

Curated biblical truth sells. Why? Because it is easy. But beware! The easier a secondary source is, the more curated and interpreted it has been. Sometimes the secondary source is right, but not always. Make no mistake: you give interpretation away at your own peril. Don't blindly trust what other people tell you about the Bible! Well-intentioned people misinterpret the Bible all the time, and the devil himself twists it to serve his own deceptive purposes. "Easier" always comes with strings attached!

TIPS AND STRATEGIES FOR STUDYING DEEP

Our goal in studying God's Word deeply is to know God better for ourselves and be transformed by His Spirit. So let's jump in and consider some simple tips, strategies, and cautions as we start to go deep in God's Word.

GO DEEP STRATEGY
Pick Translation, Not a Paraphrase

If you've ever read a version of the Bible that is "easier," don't forget that it comes with strings attached. *Easier* in translation world means that someone else has done the hard work of interpretation for you. I know this is unpopular to say, but it is true.

Translations of the Bible that stay as close to the original languages as possible are a little harder to read because the translators don't make all of the interpretative decisions for their readers. They simply do their best to translate words as closely as they can from the original languages to the target language.

While I read different translations as well as an occasional paraphrase, when I study I stick to Bible translations that are as true as possible to the original languages. I also study in the original languages to the extent that I can—I'm far better in Greek than Hebrew. Better English translations for study are the New American Standard 95 (NASB95), the English Standard Version (ESV), and the New King James Version (NKJV).

So when you read that New Living Translation (NLT) and it is as clear as day, it is because the translators have done the work of interpretation to make what they think is the meaning of the text clear to you. The potential problem enters when translators make a text appear crystal clear that is not at all clear in the original language. This leaves the reader at risk of trusting a faulty interpretation; it is dangerous business to build our belief system on others' interpretations and opinions.

If the text is difficult in places, so be it. Better to accept that some things aren't as clear as we'd like them rather than to have a translator present a clear but wrong reading. Realize, too, that most of the Bible *is* clear. The core of the Bible, the message of the gospel, is entirely clear. We don't need to become unduly frightened over difficult passages because what we need to know, we know.

GO DEEP STRATEGY

Realize That My Lack of Understanding Does Not Render Something Untrue

A truth I've come to realize over time is this: just because I can't understand or replicate something does not mean that it is not true. Take, for instance, sending a man to the moon. With slide rules and tenacity, the United States sent men to the moon in the 1960s. I believe that it happened, I believe that we (human beings) could do it again, but I do not understand the science, physics, engineering, and so forth needed to make that happen. Even given the budget and physical resources, I would not be able to put a person on the moon because of my mental limitations in the science department.

My limitations, though, don't mean that it can't be done. It simply means that I cannot do it. It is beyond *me,* not beyond possibility. That is how I am able to handle tension with colliding truths in Scripture. Is God sovereign? Yes, absolutely. Is man responsible for his actions? He is. Do I understand how these work together? I do not. Do I believe they do? Yes, I do.

We can easily get hung up, sidetracked, and in unnecessary fights over these "difficulties" and find ourselves pulled off mission. We need to read the Bible the way we eat fish. When we come upon a bone, we just lift it out, lay it aside, and go on eating. When we come upon a "bone" in Scripture, we do the same. We lay it aside and go on reading. I may find the answer further on in my study, or I may simply have to leave it with God. After all, He is omniscient, and I am not. The fact that I cannot understand some of these apparent truth collisions helps me accept the fact that God is far greater than I am and He is worthy of my trust.

You will also find that the more you read (if you are reading with an open mind) the less you will find yourself holding onto the dogma of men. When we don't know the truth for ourselves, when we've simply memorized what we've been taught, we often cling to man's teaching because we long for something that is true and stable. We'll fight for positions that we know nothing of firsthand because we so desire security and stability. When you get into the Word of God for yourself, you find the source of truth and the dogmas of man no longer hold their importance and power. As Jesus says in the Gospel of John, ". . . and you will know the truth, and the truth will make you free" (John 8:32).

GO DEEP STRATEGY

Be Careful With Resources

As we dig deep, we need to be careful with resources because many will make interpretive decisions on our behalf. Use Bible resources, for sure, but use them wisely. Here are some examples of resources you need to handle with care and discernment because interpretation is baked into the cake:

- Chronological Bibles
- Gospel harmonies
- Any form of Bible recaps or overviews
- Commentaries

Now, as I write this, you may be thinking, "Isn't that the pot calling the kettle black?" If you're thinking this, you'd be right. As a teacher, I do my fair share of recapping and overviewing the text of Scripture. And all I can say to you is this: don't trust me *carte blanche* and don't trust any other teacher either. We are all fallible. Use the helps of people to get into the Word for yourself and always check teachers and pastors you listen to against Scripture for yourself.

> *You will not fall in love with the Word of God and the God of the Word from a distance. You need to be in the Word for yourself!*

We often convince ourselves that because other people are more learned or better trained that we should just take their word about what the Bible says. There is nothing that could be further from the truth.

You will not fall in love with the Word of God and the God of the Word from a distance. You need to be in the Word for yourself!

GO DEEP STRATEGY
Join a Class Where You Will Learn the Basics of Inductive Bible Study

Reading through the Bible will help you gain an understanding of the Bible's big picture, of the lay of the land; it will help you with context and help you see how the parts of the Bible relate to one another and hold together. As you read widely, you'll learn to hear God's voice, and it will strengthen your relationship with Him. It is His Word, and His Word truly is life to us.

In order to thoroughly digest it, though, we also need to learn to study it deeply. In his letter to Timothy, Paul writes, "Be diligent to present yourself approved to God as a workman who does not need to be ashamed, accurately handling the word of truth" (2 Timothy 2:15). A solid biblically based inductive study will help you in doing just this.

GO DEEP STRATEGY
The Basics of Inductive Study

For some people, "study" is not a comfortable word. It is, nonetheless, vital to a growing relationship with God. A good study will help you learn how to **observe, interpret,** and **apply** the text of Scripture.

These are the basics of inductive study, which simply describes a study process that uses the Bible itself as the primary source of information about the Bible instead of going to secondary sources first. Seems obvious, but you'd be amazed at how often people go sniffing around the edges of the Bible and accessing secondary source material rather than opening up the Word itself for themselves!

As we do whenever we come to the Word of God, inductive study starts with prayer, asking God to help us see and understand what He has given us in the text of Scripture. Then we get about the business of observing, interpreting, and applying.

Observation seeks to answer the question *What does the text say?* Observing the text primarily involves slowing down and learning to ask questions stemming from the basic journalistic 5 Ws and H—*Who? What? When? Where? Why?* and *How?*

As you learn to study you'll start to instinctively ask basic observation questions like:

- *Who wrote the text?*
- *Who was the text written to?*
- *What kind of literature is this?*
- *Where is the action taking place?*
- *When are the events occurring?*
- *Why was this book written?*
- *What are the key words that will help me understand the content?*
- *What is the theme of the book? Of the individual chapters?*

With each verse you'll learn to ask appropriate questions and follow-up questions just as you do in a conversation. The key to observing the text is simply slowing down and paying attention. In a world that venerates speed, pumping the brakes and slowing down—while simple in theory—can be wildly challenging. Interpretation and application start with accurate observation of the text.

Interpretation seeks to answer the question *What does the text mean?* People often confuse observation with interpretation. Let me clear this up for you with one simple question: *Have you ever been misinterpreted?* Has anyone ever misunderstood something that you've said?

If I were a betting girl (I'm not, raised Baptist . . .), I'd push all my chips in on this one for every single person who has ever lived. We have all been misinterpreted at some point in our lives. Misinterpretation causes everything from minor spats and inconveniences to major family breakdowns, divorces, and even wars.

The key to interpretation both in life and literature is context. Great harm has been done both unwittingly and intentionally when people wrest words from the Bible out of context. A favorite phrase that I learned in my days at Precept Ministries is this: *Context is king because it rules in matters of interpretation!* We can't make sense of words in isolation. We need to pay attention to their environments. In the Bible, words make up sentences, sentences group into verses, verses to chapters, and chapters to books. Context pays attention both to the words close by (near context), as well as to the teaching of Scripture as a whole (extended context). When we have a practice of regularly reading widely, we set ourselves up for success in this area.

> *During the interpretation phase of study, we are looking for the one clear meaning of the text.*

During the interpretation phase of study, we are looking for the one clear meaning of the text. This is not a "What does it mean to you?" process. Interpretation assumes that the author intends to deliver a specific message to a specific audience. As an author myself, I decide meaning and try to communicate it to my readers. If I'm not clear or if I use a term that you're not familiar with, you may misinterpret what I mean, but it doesn't change my intent.

As we interpret Scripture, we aim to discover the one clear meaning of the text. This always involves paying attention to context. Often it means we'll be doing work on original language words (Hebrew for the Old Testament or Greek for the New Testament) in order to discover word meaning with more clarity. Fortunately, the internet makes this easy today. Sometimes cross-references with other portions of Scripture will help us better understand the text in question.

We remember that Scripture is the best commentary on Scripture and will never contradict itself. While interpretation may sound like a difficult process, most of Scripture is clear and readily understandable.

When James, for instance, starts writing about the mouth, I understand him immediately and completely.

James 3:4-8

4   *Look at the ships also, though they are so great and are driven by strong winds, are still directed by a very small rudder wherever the inclination of the pilot desires.*

5   *So also the tongue is a small part of the body, and yet it boasts of great things. See how great a forest is set aflame by such a small fire!*

6   *And the tongue is a fire, the very world of iniquity; the tongue is set among our members as that which defiles the entire body, and sets on fire the course of our life, and is set on fire by hell.*

7   *For every species of beasts and birds, of reptiles and creatures of the sea, is tamed and has been tamed by the human race.*

8   *But no one can tame the tongue; it is a restless evil and full of deadly poison.*

James makes his case clearly about the tongue. I can't tame my tongue, only God can do that in me through His Spirit. I know what James says and means almost immediately; my issue with James isn't understanding, my issue is application . . . which leads us to the final component of inductive study.

Application asks *How can I apply the clear meaning of the text in my life?*

Truth be told, a great temptation in Bible study is to stop the process after answering the observation and interpretation questions. For those of us with an academic bent, we get the academic high of the answers and often decide to call it a day, particularly if we're not directly prompted or challenged to diligently apply the Word and seek the Lord on how to live it out.

The biblical Pharisees picture for us those who observed and interpreted the text of Scripture but did not live out its precepts from the heart. They are some of the most tragic figures in the biblical text garnering "woe" after "woe" from Jesus.

To observe and interpret the text of Scripture without applying it is nothing short of biblical studies malpractice. In fact, the older I get the more convinced I become that the people who should be most thrilled that we are studying the Bible are those closest to us. Our spouses, children, neighbors, friends, and co-workers should rejoice that we are studying the Bible because of the collateral affect it has on them as God causes us to look and behave more and more like Jesus. Think about it.

GO DEEP STRATEGY
Don't Fall Into These Pits

As we study deeply and move toward actionable truth, pressure can build to make something of what we see—and we can be tempted to do that in our own power. Here are three pitfalls to avoid:

1. Avoid the temptation to spiritualize.

Have you ever sat in a "Bible study" (and, yes, the quotation marks are deliberate) where everyone in the group takes a turn telling what a particular passage "means to them"? Almost all of us have. This is one way that we do not accurately handle the Word of Truth. Yes, the Bible speaks to us today, but that speaking must come out of and be grounded in an understanding of what the text said to its original hearers. What it means to us comes out of what it meant.

Now, I am aware that often what people actually mean when they ask "What does this mean to you?" is "How are you applying the meaning of this text in your life?"

Still, we need to realize that the text has meaning apart from our interaction with it. As we study Scripture we seek to interpret the one clear meaning of the text—what it meant to the original hearers. Our application, how we apply the text—which will be very personal and often varied—will be grounded in the text's clear meaning.

We spiritualize when we divorce our current application from the text's original meaning and allow any wind of emotion to toss us on the waves.

2. Avoid the temptation to naturalize.

On the other extreme is the temptation to naturalize the Bible, that is to disallow anything that is not empirical, anything that cannot be seen, measured, touched, felt, examined, or proved. According to a naturalistic view, miracles could not have happened because they do not fit the way we know the world operates. Great fish do not swallow and vomit people. Angels do not appear on earth. People do not rise from the dead. Therefore, accordingly, Jesus could not have been raised from the dead; neither could He have raised others. Miracles are defined as impossible and eyewitness accounts deemed noncredible.

By this standard, Jesus could not have walked on water unless that water was below 32 degrees Fahrenheit, and fives loaves of bread and two fish could never have fed 5,000 men (to say nothing of their dates).

Now, while many would not think of viewing the New Testament in a naturalistic way, the Old Testament is quite another story. It is not uncommon to find people who accept the miracles of Jesus but can't bring themselves to believe that a big fish swallowed a cantankerous prophet named Jonah. Similarly, they accept Jesus as God but can't accept that God may actually have made the earth in six days.

111

Certainly, the Bible uses figurative language at times: the Psalms, Revelation, and the prophets are some examples. And when figurative language is used, we need to interpret the material in the manner that the author intended. That said, we cannot force the term "figurative language" or "allegory" on people or events that Jesus spoke of as being real. If you're feeling disagreeable here, just consider what I'm saying; write me a note in the margin and move on. I'm not dying on this hill, but it is something to think about.

3. Avoid the temptation to dogmatize.

If you grew up in the church, you probably struggle with this problem to some degree whether or not you're aware of it and own it. Dogmatizing makes the Bible agree with a view that you already hold as opposed to letting Scripture speak for itself.

For example, you will approach the Bible differently if you consider yourself an Arminian than you will if you consider yourself a five- or seven-point Calvinist. To put this much more simply, if you bring a preconceived notion that man can lose his salvation, you will handle the text differently than if you assume that believers are eternally secure. If you believe that predestination and free will are a one-or-the-other proposition, this will affect the way that you interpret the Bible.

Your church may have pet views on the rapture of the church, modes of baptism, what actually happens during the Lord's Supper, or any one of a number of other things. Because of the views that surround us and our own preconceived ideas, the tendency to read into (*eisiogesis*) the Bible what we think it says can be strong. We all have presuppositions. If we say that we don't, we are lying or naive.

Presuppositions don't destine us to failure in Bible study. Still, we need to be aware of what they are and keep them in check as we come to the Bible so that we position ourselves to be corrected by the Holy Spirit where we need it. The more we allow the Bible to speak for itself and to interpret itself—remember, Scripture is the best interpreter of Scripture—the better off we will be.

Furthermore, choosing between two opposing views or dogmas may put us on a wrong path. Some combined biblical truth (such as the sovereignty of God and the responsibility of man) may not make sense to us, but they do to God. By faith I accept both, let God solve the apparent dilemma, and move on in my study of the Bible.

GO DEEP STRATEGY

Understand and Value Context in Deep Study

Studying deeply without context is near impossible unless you constantly rely on someone else to point you to cross-references. Many good inductive studies provide this service. You study the text and the workbook tells you where to go for similar material. You will build knowledge this way over time, but it keeps you tied to a middleman to show you the connections. When you read widely for yourself, you open the door to seeing those connections for yourself in the long term; in the short term, you'll be better able to weigh and evaluate the cross-references studies provide to you.

You're doing great with your reading here! In fact, we're about halfway through! Let's put this book down and get back into The Book for awhile. Remember, that's the whole point of what we're doing here. We'll look at some more tips and strategies for deep study again in the next chapter.

DRAW NEAR THIS WEEK

Pick one or more of the opportunities for drawing near. Feel free to continue with what you have been reading or try a new book.

- Start or continue reading the Gospel of John to help you begin building the habit of daily fixing your eyes on Jesus.
- Start reading in 1 Samuel if you're already a pro in Genesis. Remember to put your pencil down and try to read in increments of at least 30 minutes as you're building your reading habit.
- Start reading in Genesis if you've never read it before.
- Pick one or two of the following shorter epistles to read in one sitting: Galatians, Ephesians, Philippians, or Colossians.
- Dig deeply into Psalm 100 using the inductive study questions on the following pages.

Psalm 100

A Psalm for Thanksgiving.

1 *Shout joyfully to the L*ORD*, all the earth.*
2 *Serve the L*ORD *with gladness;*
 Come before Him with joyful singing.
3 *Know that the L*ORD *Himself is God;*
 It is He who has made us, and not we ourselves;
 We are His people and the sheep of His pasture.
4 *Enter His gates with thanksgiving*
 And His courts with praise.
 Give thanks to Him, bless His name.
5 *For the L*ORD *is good;*
 His lovingkindness is everlasting
 And His faithfulness to all generations.

OBSERVATION

READ the text and **MARK** every reference to the LORD, including synonyms and pronouns. LIST what the text tells about the LORD. (*Who*)

READ the psalm again and **MARK** any words that give information about the author. LIST what you learn. (*Who*)

READ the psalm again, noting what the relationship is between God and the people. (*What*)

READ the psalm again and note everything the psalmist instructs his readers to do or know. (*What*)

What phrases in the text point us to location? What is it? (*Where*)

Why is the location significant? (*Why*)

What time phrases did you notice? (*When*)

What do they tell us about God? Why are they significant? (*What* and *Why*)

How are the people to interact with God? (*How*)

INTERPRETATION

What is the context of this psalm? What was the purpose?

What is the Hebrew word translated "lovingkindness," and how is it used throughout the Old Testament? How can this help us understand this text better?

What about the Hebrew word translated "faithfulness"?

What should the hearers have understood about the LORD from this psalm?

APPLICATION

What did you learn about God from this psalm?

Is there anything in this psalm that challenges the way that you think about God? Anything that challenges the way you interact with or act toward Him?

DISCUSS TOGETHER

These questions can be used in a discussion group if you're using this book in a Bible study setting or book club. You can also use them to process through what you're learning on your own.

- Where have you been reading in the Word this week?
  - How has it been going?
  - What have been your biggest takeaways?
  - What questions have you had that may need further study?
- What new strategies have you been trying this week?
  - What has worked?
  - What strategies are you thinking about trying this week?
- Do you have any previous experience with inductive Bible study?
  - If so, what did you think?
  - If not, what do you think of the approach?
  - How can you start applying inductive principles to difficult passages you encounter when reading widely?
- What did you learn as you slowed down to work your way through Psalm 100?
  - What did you learn about the Lord? About yourself?
- What concerns do you need to bring to the Lord this week with regard to His Word?

READ TOGETHER

If you're meeting with a group, spend some of your time reading the Bible aloud. This week take turns reading selected **psalms**. Focus on what each teaches about God and identify key words and themes. You can pick your own favorites or read some of these well-known chapters:

- Psalm 1
- Psalm 19
- Psalm 22
- Psalm 23
- Psalm 27
- Psalm 37
- Psalm 46
- Psalm 51
- Psalm 63
- Psalm 100
- Psalm 121
- Psalm 139

When you're finished reading and/or listening, pray for one another that God will continue to reveal Himself to you through His Word and by His Spirit.

CHAPTER 6

More Strategies for Studying Deeply

Plus Some Passages for Practice

WHILE YOU MAY RUN INTO SLIGHTLY DIFFERENT study methods and terminology, all good Bible study will be based around exegesis and hermeneutics. Exegesis means "to lead out." In other words, it is the practice of letting the text speak for itself, of drawing the meaning from what is there—no more, no less. Hermeneutics is the art and science of interpreting Scripture. While exegesis is the practice of determining what the message was to the original audience through observation and interpretation, hermeneutics deals with the principles used to interpret. As mentioned in the section on inductive Bible study in Chapter 5, while Scripture can be applied in many ways to many situations, valid application is anchored in and emerges from the one clear meaning of the text.

Because we look to determine the one clear meaning of the text as we study, we can sometimes find ourselves discouraged when we encounter less-than-clear passages from time to time. The good news is that most of the Bible is clear, but for what isn't immediately obvious there is hope! There is always hope!

Remember, No One "Gets" Everything Right Away

If you're the kind of person who's bothered whenever you don't understand something, take a breath. No one gets everything right away, not even you. I hate it, too, but it's true. Often we simply need to keep reading, keep praying, and keep watching before we see connections. Occasionally, we find ourselves having to declare "Oh, great mystery!" but those times are rare.

God has revealed much that we can understand through creation (Romans 1/Psalm 19), more as the author of Hebrews says as He spoke "long ago to the fathers in the prophets in many portions and in many ways" (we read of this throughout the Old Testament), and still more through His Son (Hebrews 1:1), but He has not revealed everything. Moses writes in Deuteronomy 29:29 that "The secret things belong to the LORD our God, but the things revealed belong to us and to our sons forever, that we may observe all the words of this law."

Be encouraged! The better we come to know our good Heavenly Father, the easier is becomes to tolerate mystery when we encounter it and to trust Him with all of the secret things because we know that He is good and does good and causes all things to work together for good to those who love Him and are the called according to His purpose (Psalm 119:68/Romans 8:28).

Apply the Clear and Live in Light of It

If we're honest, it's not the one percent or five percent or even ten percent of the Bible that we don't understand that poses the problem for us; it is the ninety-nine percent, ninety-five percent, or ninety percent that we do understand that gets in our kitchen. Sure, we can all come up with a few head-scratchers in Scripture, but how much would alternate interpretations actually affect the way we live? Usually, not at all.

Conversely, how different would the visible church look today if regular attendees loved and pursued God through His Word and were being transformed from the inside out into people who love the brethren, who pursue peace with all people, who let their lights shine, who walk in the light, who hold marriage in honor, who are neither shackled by the love of money nor live in slavery to the fear of death? I trust you see my point.

How different would the church at large look if we followed Paul's instructions to Titus on how older men, older women, younger men, and younger women should live? When I'm tempted to fuss over the obscure unclear, I remind myself of how much of the crystal clear I could start applying instead.

GO DEEP STRATEGY

Always Start with the Clear When You're Confused

Whenever I find myself confused by a passage of Scripture, I read and re-read and re-read some more. Then, I slow down and start by framing the passage with what is clear instead of beginning with what is unclear or seems problematic.

Let me give you an example of a passage that fell hard on my ears for years; maybe it has on yours, too. Matthew recounts an interaction with a Gentile woman after Jesus and the disciples withdraw from the Galilee to the region of Tyre and Sidon. I'll ask you to read this and jot down your initial thoughts, then we can go back and start to frame some clear facts that we tend to overlook. Again, for context, Jesus and the disciples are moving from a Jewish area into a Gentile region when we pick up this text.

Matthew 15:21-28

21 *Jesus went away from there, and withdrew into the district of Tyre and Sidon.*

22 *And a Canaanite woman from that region came out and began to cry out, saying, "Have mercy on me, Lord, Son of David; my daughter is cruelly demon-possessed."*

23 *But He did not answer her a word. And His disciples came and implored Him, saying, "Send her away, because she keeps shouting at us."*

24 *But He answered and said, "I was sent only to the lost sheep of the house of Israel."*

25 *But she came and began to bow down before Him, saying, "Lord, help me!"*

26 *And He answered and said, "It is not good to take the children's bread and throw it to the dogs."*

27 *But she said, "Yes, Lord; but even the dogs feed on the crumbs which fall from their masters' table."*

28 *Then Jesus said to her, "O woman, your faith is great; it shall be done for you as you wish." And her daughter was healed at once.*

Does this passage elicit any emotional response from you? Unless you've spent some time with it and worked through it in the past, I'm going to guess it does. If so, go ahead and jot down your response below.

Perhaps because I am not only a woman, but also a Gentile woman and a mother, I strongly relate with the woman who is seeking help from

Jesus. I have an almost visceral reaction against what seems to be heartlessness here among the disciples who don't want to be bothered, and I'm initially confused by Jesus' response. He eventually helps the woman, but the delay seems to indicate there is more to the story. Often we feel these "feels" and move on with a bad taste in our mouths about the disciples and feeling a little off balance about Jesus, too.

If we resist the urge to run away from this passage, we can frame in pieces that are clear that can help us understand parts that are less clear or unsettling.

Let's start with these questions to help us from the information:

- *Who are the people involved in this passage?*
- *What do we know about the woman? What does her address of Jesus as the "Son of David" indicate?*
- *What do the disciples want Jesus to do with her? Does He listen to them?*
- *What does Jesus say about the woman and do for her?*

Let's think through our answers and see if framing some of the clear answers will help us with what is less clear. So here are clear data points from the text:

- While the core interaction is between Jesus and the woman, the disciples are involved. They are listening, watching, and even weighing in on how Jesus should respond to the woman.
- The Gentile woman recognizes Jesus as the Jewish Messiah. We see this in her address of Him as the "Son of David." The outsider has inside information.
- The disciples want the woman gone and they implore Jesus to send her away. The "good guys" are acting like "bad guys."
- Jesus refuses to send the woman away.

At this point, I think it's also important to bring to bear what we already know clearly about Jesus.

- He is good and compassionate.
- He heals both Jews and Gentiles.

- He is love.
- He will not act in sin.

Knowing that Jesus, simply by nature of who He is, would not treat the woman sinfully, we rule out some potential interpretations.

Without belaboring this point, knowing that Jesus is entirely good, that the disciples seem to be having a bad moment, and they are interacting with a woman who has clear faith, my best guess is that this is not only an opportunity for Jesus to heal a little girl, but also a teaching moment for the disciples where Jesus gave this woman an opportunity to show her great faith as an example to them.

Could I be wrong? Sure, on part of it. What I am not wrong on, however, is Jesus. He loves the woman. He is good and compassionate and has come to seek and save the lost . . . of the house of Israel and the world at large . . . and that, ultimately, guides me through this otherwise tough passage. When something is not immediately clear, don't panic! Start with what you can know and do know, and go from there.

GO DEEP STRATEGY

Keep Praying!

Don't forget to ask God! We pray for the desire to read. We pray as we read for understanding. We pray when we come across difficult passages that God will teach us what we need to know! Remember Psalm 119:102 where the psalmist writes, "I have not turned aside from Your precepts, for You Yourself have taught me." When you're stuck, pray!

GO DEEP STRATEGY

Don't Be Snared by Reading *About* the Bible Instead of Going to the Primary Source for Yourself!

This is an easy trap to fall into. I know because I spent a good part of my college years here. Reading commentaries and other secondary sources provides credible help in Bible study after you've done your own work.

Once you've prayed and studied for yourself, commentaries can help confirm your findings and sometimes alert you to points you may have overlooked. If you live in the commentaries and not the Word, however, they will simply confuse you because when the commentaries disagree, you will not have the discernment to know which is right.

The life-changing power of God comes when we directly interact with Him through His Word. Commentators, while helpful, simply are not inspired. The Bible, conversely, describes itself rightly as "God-breathed" (2 Timothy 3:16). Should you use commentaries when you are studying in-depth? Absolutely, but consult them *after* you've done your own work, *after* you've wrestled with the text yourself in study and prayer. You will be more informed and better able to judge the value of what the commentators say about a passage if you have first done the work yourself.

A couple of other points on commentaries worth noting: first, make sure that you use more than one commentary so you can compare viewpoints; second, take care to choose a reputable commentator, one who tells you all the alternate views of interpretation before letting you know why he has chosen his particular view. Other helps in selecting a commentary can be the advice of a pastor or teacher in your church or taking note of the publisher.

GO DEEP STRATEGY
Major on the Majors

The ungodly will major on the minors. The Bible teaches this clearly. Paul writes in 2 Timothy 2:23, "But refuse foolish and ignorant speculations, knowing that they produce quarrels." The ungodly argue about genealogies and details and, well, weird stuff. They make extra rules, force people to jump through hoops, and generally steer people away from the simple gospel. They elevate unclear passages, building them up into major tenets of the faith while at the same time totally missing the mark on clear truths, specifically the person and work of Jesus Christ.

Ask "Is this prescriptive or descriptive?"

The Bible is packed with accounts of sinful people interacting with a perfect God. Because of this we often see even biblical protagonists—the "good guys"—behaving badly. Critics may point to the Bible and say, "Hey, Jacob had multiple wives! How do you follow a God who condones that?" Here we see an example of a descriptive text. Jacob did have more than one wife and the text describes how it came about. He sought to marry Rachel, but his father-in-law tricked him into marrying Leah, her older sister, and then allowed him to marry Rachel also. Is polygamy prescriptive in the Bible, that is, is it something prescribed or commanded by Scripture? Absolutely not. The Bible describes and reports on polygamous relationships but prescribes monogamy. Genesis 2:24 gives us prescriptive teaching about marriage, and it involves one man and one woman:

Genesis 2:24

24   For this reason a man shall leave his father and his mother, and be joined to his wife; and they shall become one flesh.

In the New Testament, Paul quotes Genesis and expands the teaching to show that marriage also is a picture of Christ and the church. He writes this in Ephesians 5:

Ephesians 5:31-33

31   FOR THIS REASON A MAN SHALL LEAVE HIS FATHER AND MOTHER AND SHALL BE JOINED TO HIS WIFE, AND THE TWO SHALL BECOME ONE FLESH.

32   This mystery is great; but I am speaking with reference to Christ and the church.

33   Nevertheless, each individual among you also is to love his own wife even as himself, and the wife must see to it that she respects her husband.

The prescriptive teaching on marriage is one man and one woman, but throughout the Old Testament we see descriptions of behavior that deviate from God's clear command. We also see the collateral damage that follows as people walk in their own ways and do what is right in their own eyes.

GO DEEP STRATEGY

Another Example of Descriptive

We see descriptive text throughout the Bible, particularly in heavily narrative sections. Another clear example appears in Judges 6 where Gideon lays out a fleece asking God to confirm what He has spoken in order to gain direction on how to move forward.

Gideon lived during the time when judges led Israel. It was a dark time in the nation's history characterized by people doing what was right in their own eyes. Although God had delivered them from slavery in Egypt and had protected them for forty years in the wilderness, upon coming in the Promised Land the people quickly turned their hearts toward other gods.

The book of Judges records cycles of sin among the people which repeatedly brings God's judgment in the form of other nation's oppressing them. Eventually the people cry out to God who raises up a judge to deliver them from their oppressors. They follow God to some extent while the judge lives, but when the judge dies, they revert to further sin and the cycle continues.

In the midst of one of these sin cycles, God raises up Gideon to deliver the people from the oppressing Midianites. Let's pick up the text in Judges 6:

Judges 6:36-40

36 *Then Gideon said to God, "If You will deliver Israel through me, as You have spoken,*

37 *behold, I will put a fleece of wool on the threshing floor. If there is dew on the fleece only, and it is dry on all*

127

the ground, then I will know that You will deliver Israel through me, as You have spoken."

38 *And it was so. When he arose early the next morning and squeezed the fleece, he drained the dew from the fleece, a bowl full of water.*

39 *Then Gideon said to God, "Do not let Your anger burn against me that I may speak once more; please let me make a test once more with the fleece, let it now be dry only on the fleece, and let there be dew on all the ground."*

40 *God did so that night; for it was dry only on the fleece, and dew was on all the ground.*

You almost certainly have heard of someone who has set a fleece before the Lord saying it is biblical because Gideon did it.

Yes, Gideon did set a fleece before the Lord and God did answer him by it. Nowhere in Scripture, though, are we commanded or even encouraged to do likewise. This passage describes a man of weak faith asking God for reassurance. It is descriptive. God can answer by fleece if He chooses, but He most certainly is not obligated to do so.

Don't be prescriptive where God has been descriptive.

GO DEEP STRATEGY
Be Clear on the Clear

Before we move on, I need to make one qualification. While you will not understand everything you read or even study in the Bible—and that's okay for the time being—there are a few points where you need to gain clarity by pursuing them with diligence sooner rather than later.

1. YOU NEED TO BE CLEAR ON JESUS CHRIST.

Do you want to make sure that you have the main point of the Bible? Do you want to know that you won't be an easy mark for a bizarre heresy and find yourself in the headlines for "drinking the Kool-Aid"? Then get clear on the person and work of Jesus Christ. Don't fuss over things like baptism for the dead or levels of heaven. Don't argue over the 144,000 of Revelation. Stick to Jesus and make sure you are clear on Him. For a study that will guide you in this, check out *Jesus: Sweetest Name I Know.* It's a simple inductive study that will lead you through the basics about who Jesus is and why it matters.

Jesus is the place where every heretical teaching will veer off from the truth in some way, big or small. Not almost every heresy, every heresy. Read the Gospels until you understand who Jesus is, the God-man, 100% human, 100% divine. Watch how the Old Testament points to Him. Look at the sacrificial system with a view toward the ultimate sacrifice of Jesus Christ. See how the prophets point toward Him. Build on the foundation of Jesus. Get your Christology right and go from there.

2. YOU NEED TO BE CLEAR ON THE GOSPEL.

How do you have a right relationship with the God of the universe? How do you walk with Him now and into eternity? These are topics that matter. Spend as much time as you need here and come back to review often, learning to regularly preach the gospel to yourself, reminding yourself of the key truth of life.

Most people, even many who profess to believe the Bible, think that in some fashion they have to work their way to God. This, however, is not biblical. The reason the gospel is good news is that Jesus accomplishes salvation for us. When we cannot work our way to God, Jesus makes the way for us.

The word *gospel* literally means "good news" (from the Greek *euaggelion: eu,* good; *aggelion,* message). Paul writes of the good news often, but spells it out clearly and succinctly in a letter to the church at Corinth:

1 Corinthians 15:3-8

3 *For I delivered to you as of first importance what I also received, that Christ died for our sins according to the Scriptures,*

4 *and that He was buried, and that He was raised on the third day according to the Scriptures,*

5 and that He appeared to Cephas, then to the twelve.

6 After that He appeared to more than five hundred brethren at one time, most of whom remain until now, but some
have fallen asleep;

7 then He appeared to James, then to all the apostles;

8 and last of all, as to one untimely born, He appeared to me
also.

Let's take a moment to practice some of our inductive study skills.
READ the text and MARK every reference to *Christ*, including pronouns.
Then note what Paul says about what Jesus did and why.

In six succinct verses, Paul summarizes the components of the gospel of Jesus Christ.

- **Christ died** for our sins. Because Jesus Christ was without sin, He could pay the penalty for our sin.

- **He was buried.** Jesus actually died; it was not an extended faint-ing spell or ruse by the disciples. He died and was placed in a tomb guarded by Roman soldiers.

- **He was raised** on the third day. When God raised Jesus from the dead, the power of sin and death was broken. Death could not hold the perfect and sinless Son of God!

- **He appeared.** People saw the risen Christ. It was not a mere myth or legend. Eyewitnesses beheld Him—over 500. Death had been defeated!

3. YOU NEED TO BE CLEAR ON WHAT CHRIST'S DEATH ACCOMPLISHES FOR YOU.

Okay, you may say, "So He died for my sins; what practically does that mean for me?" It means that you and I can have a right relationship with God and thereby be delivered from the power of sin and of death. It means forgiveness, hope, and peace in the here and now and life everlasting in the presence of God.

As it stands, if we don't have a relationship with God, we are in deep, deep trouble. We may or may not acknowledge it, but it is true nonetheless. Look around and you'll see what happens when people are without God and without hope in this world (Ephesians 2:12).

The Bible says that we have sinned; we have missed the mark and have fallen short of what God requires, which is absolute perfection. The apostle Paul writes in Romans 3:23, "... for all have sinned and fall short of the glory of God." Mankind was created in God's image and likeness, but in our sin we have broken and twisted that image and separated ourselves from Him. In our world this is a hard concept to accept since we tend to either compare ourselves to others and think, "Well, at least I'm not as bad as that guy!" or else we reject the reality of absolute truth entirely. Think of Pilate in his interaction with Jesus when he declares, "What is truth?" (John 18:38). If truth doesn't exist, if we jettison the concept of absolute truth, how can I fall short of a standard that is not even real in the first place? Rationalization brings relief in the moment, but in the end leads straight to the pit of hell eternally and eventually to existential despair for any thinking person in the here and now.

The apostle Paul writes in Romans 3:23, "... for all have sinned and fall short of the glory of God."

Because people tend to think of themselves as essentially good, sometimes an illustration helps. The illustration that is most helpful to me is picturing God's standard by thinking of a swimming race from the coast of San Diego to the coast of Kaanapali Beach on Maui. The goal (or the standard) in this picture is clear: Hawaii.

Each of us suits up and begins on the beach in San Diego. When the gun sounds and we all jump into the water, some of us are going to make it further than others. Some will be better, others will be inferior. You might make it further than I will, but Michael Phelps will make it further than both of us (unless there is something about you that I don't know!). But make no mistake, none of us is making it to Hawaii without the assistance of a boat, plane, or helicopter. The goal is not attainable, just as the perfect standard of God is not attainable by mere human beings. Only Jesus, the One who is both fully human and fully God, was able to meet the standard that the Law set.

Some of us are better than others. Mother Teresa lived an exemplary life. Jesus Himself speaks highly of John the Baptist. Neither Mother Teresa nor John the Baptist, however, could match the perfection that God requires. No one comes to the Father except through Jesus (John 14:6).

Sorry, but before we can get to the actual good news of Jesus, the path darkens further because sin brings consequences to sinners. The Bible calls it a wage. That wage, spelled out in Romans 6:23, is death. Paul writes, "For the wages of sin is death…." This is not a good place to be. It is, however, where all humanity is apart from Christ because none of us can make that swim to Hawaii. The standard is too high, the gap between God's holiness and our sinfulness is too great.

Fortunately, God does not leave us to sink in the Pacific Ocean of sin. Instead, He reaches out to us in our corrupted condition to rescue us. Paul puts it this way in Romans 5:6, "For while we were still helpless, at the right time Christ died for the ungodly." He brings His one-person helicopter to us off the coast of San Diego (because that's how far off even the best human being is!), gets into the water, and helps us safely aboard the chopper when He becomes man and dies in our place on the cross.

132

Although Christ died for the ungodly, not all of the ungodly have accepted the gift. So, how do we practically lay hold of this cure, this rescue, that God has affected on our behalf?

The Bible tells us in Ephesians 2:8-9: "For by grace you have been saved through faith; and that not of yourselves, *it is* the gift of God; not as a result of works, so that no one may boast." The difference between intellectual assent to facts and saving faith is often illustrated by the use of a chair. You can look at a chair and theoretically believe that it will support your weight, but until you park your behind, you have not actually trusted it to sustain you.

Another illustration that may be helpful comes from the team-building arena. Years ago, my husband and I worked in youth ministry. As such, we often helped lead retreats for high schoolers. One weekend on a leadership retreat the students participated in a team-building course which involved something called a trust fall. You may be familiar with this.

One person stands on an elevated platform while the teammates stand below with their arms carefully joined to form a human net. The lucky one on the platform then falls backwards into the arms of the people below. Now each of the kids knew that the stunt would work; after all, even when you have signed a waiver, camps can't be dropping kids on the regular. Still, believing in their heads that the friends would make the catch was a million miles from falling backwards and dropping. The first is intellectual assent, the latter a picture of biblical belief or trust.

GO DEEP STRATEGY

Rejoice That You'll Never Run Out

For years after graduating from college and realizing that my professors had likely forgotten more than I will ever know about the Bible, I lamented my lack in Scriptural knowledge. I knew the truth about Jesus, I was solid on the basics of the gospel, but still it seemed at times that no matter how much I learned, there was so much more *to be* learned. Not only that, the more I learned, the more I realized I didn't know. It's one thing to suspect there's more there than you think, it's another thing to have seen it and feel your lack. I'm guessing I'm not alone in this.

We're all at different places in our spiritual growth and if we're paying attention and have any degree of humility, we have a sense of the magnitude of God and His revelation and our smallness. If you feel this way, let me affirm the attitude of humility, but let's see if we can do something about the overwhelm that often tags along for the ride.

Several years ago I had an epiphany (definition number 3 if you're looking the word up) on the final day of the *Survivor* season that has changed my outlook on biblical overwhelm. And, yes, *that Survivor*. My family is a *Survivor* family. We've been gathering together since Season 1 for what we like to refer to as Tribal Night to have pizza and watch people from across the country outwit, outplay, and outlast. Before you start to judge me on this, I first learned about *Survivor* at a Precept advanced training event where I met a woman who told me about the show. She was watching it because a young man from her church was a competitor during the first season. (For my fellow *Survivor* nerds, that young man was Dirk from Onalaska, Wisconsin.) But I digress.

Back to the story. That particular year as we were about to gather for our final Tribal Night, I thought about the relative sadness of the season being over. (I know, I think too much.) I got to thinking of other similar things that are "over." You know what I mean. Think about that book you loved and the feeling you had when you turned the final page and read the last words. There's the excitement of knowing the ending, but there's loss that comes with no more pages remaining. Same thing with the television series that ends—whether you're dealing with a cancellation or a series conclusion, there's the sense of loss of *it's over*.

As I mulled this over in my mind, I started to think of how dramatically different God's Word is, because it is never "over." Even when we've read the whole thing (even multiple times), even when we study deeply hour upon hour, we will never plumb its depths. We will never run out!

A switch flipped in my mind! I didn't punt and say, "Oh well, I'll never get it all so why try?" Instead, I realized, "I will never run out! No matter how much I study, there will always be more to learn. Nobody can fully master it!"

So if you're lamenting your lack because you "don't know everything," relax. No one does. We all have more to learn and none of us will ever run out!

GO DEEP STRATEGY

Slow Down and Ask Questions

When we're reading widely, particularly in narrative sections of the Bible, we often need to put the pencils down and pick up some speed in order to gain context and see the big picture. When we're studying, however, when we're digging deeply into a particular portion of Scripture, the key principle to remember is to simply SLOW DOWN, to read and re-read and re-read some more. Picking up the pencils and marking the text helps us to slow down.

Slowing down, though, is counter cultural. Everything in our society tells us faster, faster, faster. Before we became politically correct, mental deficits were almost always referred to in speed terms: retarded, delayed, slow. Our culture always pushes for more and fast.

In deep study, pumping the brakes is key to progress. Speed when you read, but for study go slow.

In deep study, pumping the brakes is key to progress. Speed when you read, but for study go slow.

When you slow down to observe the text of Scripture, you'll find that you need far less study prompts because you will start to see distinctives of the text for yourself. If a particular word shows up nine times in ten verses, you may not notice if you are zipping by quickly, but if you're going slowly and marking, you will. You may not notice it the first time, but when you re-read eventually you will pick it up.

When you slow down, you'll start to answer the 5 Ws and H questions naturally. Repeated words and phrases will surface. Comparisons and contrasts will stand out. You'll see terms of conclusion and time phrases. You'll notice locations, and eventually you'll be able to tell someone in simple terms what the author is saying. You'll discover the main theme or themes of the passage just like you'll eventually notice the color of the walls if you sit in a room long enough.

"But," you may say, "this has never worked for me. I've never been able to pick out a key word to save my life." My question: How long have you lingered in the passage?" Going deep in study takes time. Why not sit a little longer?

GO DEEP STRATEGY
Remember That it Takes Practice

Our instant culture trains us every day to want instant results in everything. The benefits that come from digging into the solid food of Scripture take time but are life-changing. The author of Hebrews puts it this way in Hebrews 5:13-14 as he (or she!) addresses Jewish believers who have not yet grown up: "For everyone who partakes only of milk is not accustomed to the word of righteousness, for he is an infant. But solid food is for the mature, who because of practice have their senses trained to discern good and evil." Maturity doesn't happen overnight— but with solid food and practice, believers have their senses trained to discern good and evil.

GO DEEP STRATEGY
For Help in Christian Living, Study the Book

As we seek to go deeper with God, a path forward many people choose is that of Christian living books. We love to hear from other human beings how to know God better and how to live according to His ways. Some buy books to purportedly hear the voice of God more clearly!

It's preposterous! Why would we go to the words of people in place of the Word of God? Don't settle for man's (or woman's) words when you need help in how to live. Find out what God has to say. When I find myself confused in life, I go to the Word to find out what God has to say!

Many, if not most, of the Bible studies that I've written are my journey to discover what the Bible has to say that address my questions about life issues such as worry, mentoring, materialism, loving when its hard, discernment, etc. As it turns out, people are full of answers. Unfortunately, they are often the wrong answers. If you want unadulterated truth for life, go to God's Book!

`GO DEEP STRATEGY`

Remember That the Bible is Clear

I love the words of Dr. Wayne Grudem given on the perspicuity, the clarity, of Scripture. He points out that Scripture itself affirms that it can be understood, but

- not all at once
- not without effort
- not without ordinary means
- not without the reader's willingness to obey it
- not without the help of the Holy Spirit
- not without human misunderstanding
- never completely.[7,8]

So be encouraged. Keep working. Keep obeying. Keep praying. Keep recalibrating. Keep going, because you will never run out.

---

7. The Gospel Coalition. Interpreting Scripture: A General Introduction. https://www.thegospelcoalition.org/essay/interpreting-scripture-a-general-introduction/
8. The Gospel Coalition. The Perspicuity of Scripture. https://www.thegospelcoalition.org/themelios/article/the-perspicuity-of-scripture/

DRAW NEAR THIS WEEK

Pick one or more of the opportunities for drawing near. Feel free to continue with what you have been reading or try a new book.

- Start or continue reading the Gospel of John to help you begin building the habit of daily fixing your eyes on Jesus.
- Start reading in 1 Samuel if you're already a pro in Genesis. Remember to put your pencil down and aim to read in increments of at least 30 minutes as you're building your reading habit.
- Start reading in Genesis if you've never read it before.
- Pick one or two of the following shorter epistles to read in one sitting: Galatians, Ephesians, Philippians, or Colossians.
- Get a bookmark and start reading in the Psalms. This book will take almost five hours to read, so I suggest reading it concurrently with other books so you don't get overwhelmed or feel stuck.

DISCUSS TOGETHER

These questions can be used in a discussion group if you're using this book in a Bible study setting or book club. You can also use them to process through what you're learning on your own.

- Where have you been reading in the Word this week?
  - How has it been going?
  - What have been your biggest takeaways?
  - What are you specifically applying in your life?
  - What questions have you had that may need further study?
- What new strategies have you been trying this week?
  - What has worked?
  - What strategies are you thinking about trying this week?
- What do you like most about reading widely?
  - How are you improving in your reading?
  - What challenges remain?
- What do you like most about studying deeply?
  - How are you improving in your study?
  - What challenges remain?
- What concerns do you need to bring to the Lord this week with regard to His Word? What other concerns do you need to bring to Him?

READ TOGETHER

If you're meeting with a group, spend some of your time reading the Bible aloud. This week take turns reading from the book of **Proverbs**. Start at the beginning and read chapter by chapter as time allows. Always remember that reading aloud is for those who want to participate. Those who prefer to listen are always welcome to follow along as others in the group read. When you're finished reading, spend some time praying for one another.

CHAPTER 7

You Can Memorize!

Going Deep With Memorization and Meditation

THE AMOUNT OF INFORMATION EACH OF US HAS at our fingertips was unthinkable to nearly everyone just 30 years ago. The computing power of the smartphone in your pocket far exceeds what NASA used to put a man on the moon back in the 1960s. Sit with that for a minute.

What does this have to do with Bible study? Quite a bit, if we're thinking. In days past—and, yes, I realize I'm dating myself here—those of us within a generation of Steve Jobs memorized information simply to make life easier. Everyone knew their own phone number and the phone numbers of close family and friends. Even now, I can give you the last 4 digits on some friends' phone numbers growing up, -8099, -4294. Depending on your age, you probably can, too. We knew each others' phone numbers because we dialed them often enough to remember them, often in spite of ourselves.

I'm embarrassed to say that while I can tell you my parents' phone numbers and that of my husband, my kids and their spouses are on speed dial. I never dial Katie or Jackie; Siri does that for me. By the time my kids had phones, the way society handled information had undergone a seismic shift.

Many of us today no longer remember physical addresses because instead of sending cards, we tend to send emails. Phone numbers? We don't waste our mental hard drive space on those. We fuss much less over spelling because spell-check fills the gaps—sort of! Almost any random fact that we could ever imagine needing or wanting, we can retrieve in seconds and easily. No longer forced to rely on libraries or microfiche (Google it!) for information, we simply say "Hey" to Siri or Alexa and seven devices within earshot compete to answer first.

While the veracity of the specific quote is questioned because no one seems to be able to pin down the original source, Albert Einstein is widely cited as having said, "Never memorize something that you can easily look up." Whether or not it goes back to Einstein, we have become a people who live by this maxim.

Now you may be thinking, "Pam, let's move on to the next chapter. Surely we have everything we need today at our fingertips . . . even Einstein says so!" I will grant you that I no longer bother memorizing verse numbers, because I can easily look those up if I need to be that specific.

Memorizing Scripture, though, involves so much more than simple information retrieval. Neither is it about performance or recitation.

> *Memorizing Scripture, though, involves so much more than simple information retrieval.*

Scripture memory is a powerful way to engage in the biblical discipline of meditating on God's Word. Please note, I am not making the case that it is the only way to meditate on God's Word. Certainly there are other ways to meditate. Memorizing is one way, and I will focus on this particular way as God has used it in my life to change me.

Before we move into more tips and strategies, let's start by looking at a stanza from Psalm 119 that extols the practices of meditating on

God's Word. Psalm 119, as you probably remember, is the longest chapter of the Bible at a robust 176 verses. What you may not know is that it is designed to be memorized.

An acrostic poem, Psalm 119 patterns around the twenty-two consonants of the Hebrew language. Thus, it breaks into twenty-two stanzas of eight lines apiece. The first word of each line corresponds to the alphabet (that is, the Aleph-Bet), and almost every line contains a reference to the Word of God as the psalmist uses eight synonyms to describe the Word. Again, while all 176 are designed, in a sense, for easy memorization in Hebrew, we'll stick to the Beth stanza for our purposes today, that is Psalm 119:9-16.

Psalm 119:9-16

9 *How can a young man keep his way pure?*
By keeping it *according to Your word.*

10 *With all my heart I have sought You;*
Do not let me wander from Your commandments.

11 *Your word I have treasured in my heart,*
That I may not sin against You.

12 *Blessed are You, O Lord;*
Teach me Your statutes.

13 *With my lips I have told of*
All the ordinances of Your mouth.

14 *I have rejoiced in the way of Your testimonies,*
As much as in all riches.

15 *I will meditate on Your precepts*
And regard Your ways.

16 *I shall delight in Your statutes;*
I shall not forget Your word.

Take a moment and reread this stanza and mark every reference to the Word of God. You should find one reference in every verse, two in verse 16 when you include synonyms (word, commandment, law, testimonies, statutes, ordinances, precepts). Go ahead and jot down what you learn.

After talking about the blessed man who walks a blameless way in Psalm 119:1-8, the opening stanza of this psalm, the psalmist asks and considers how he can be such a man as he poses and answers the question: "How can a young man keep his way pure?" It is a great question for today: How can a person—young or old, man or woman—keep their way pure? The psalmist's answer: "By keeping it according to Your word."

He then shows his readers how he will apply himself to this, saying:

- Your word I have treasured in my heart, v. 11.
  - The psalmist does this so that he will not sin against God. He knows the word and thinks on it.

The psalmist continues describing more actions he has taken or will take with regard to the Word:

- I have rejoiced in the way of Your testimonies, v. 14
- I will meditate on your precepts, v. 15a
- [I will] regard your ways, v. 15b
- I shall delight in your statutes, v. 16a
- I shall not forget your word, v. 16b.

To *treasure* in the heart, to *meditate,* and to *not forget* all point to intentional remembering and dwelling on God's Word with the purpose of following in His ways. The psalmist charts a course we would do well to follow, not of rote obedience but with a heart inclined to the Word of God and the God of the Word. Are you ready?!

GO DEEP STRATEGY
You're Not Too Old

In case you're on the fence about skipping this section and moving on, let me assure that you are not too old for this! Is memorizing harder as you age? Yes. Science and experience show us that younger brains can pack in more information faster and more efficiently. When my brain was young, fast, and wildly efficient, I thought that older people who said memorizing was too hard were just lazy. Now that I'm in that category, I've repented of that attitude. I know firsthand that it is harder for me to memorize now than when I was 25. And yet, over the years of practice, I've discovered memory techniques and strategies that work for me and compensate in areas where I used to rely on sheer "hard drive speed."

> *I've learned that as memorizing becomes more difficult, my ability to meditate deeply on the Word has increased because I need to think more purposefully about what I'm encoding in my brain and treasuring in my heart.*

Most importantly, I've learned that as memorizing becomes more difficult, my ability to meditate deeply on the Word has increased because I need to think more purposefully about what I'm encoding in my brain and treasuring in my heart. That's not a bad trade-off!

GO DEEP STRATEGY
Save Your Hard Drive Space

When you're memorizing passages, save your mental hard drive space for the words of Scripture and chapter numbers only. If you need to find your way to a particular verse, you can do that quickly enough with a visual scan or Google search. Recovering perfectionists . . . I'm talking to you! Trying to memorize specific verse numbers in passages adds unneeded complexity that will be at cross-purposes to your goal.

Pick a Translation and Stick with It

When I was child, the King James Version was the only game in town so I grew up memorizing the *thees* and *thous* of the Authorized Version. Because my childhood was filled with prizes for memorizing—from AWANA trophies to other incentives in Vacation Bible School—by the time newer translations emerged on the scene, I was already hundreds of verses invested in King James.

In my early 20s I realized I had a decision to make. Stick with "The King" or move to a more modern translation. I decided to shift to the New American Standard. I memorized in the 1975 NASB, and when the 1995 came out I moved toward that with new verses as the changes between those versions were minor. I have no plans to adapt to the NASB 2020.

I know some people who memorize different verses in different translations and find value in that, but unless you have strong convictions to this end, I'd encourage you to pick one translation and stick with it for your memorizing adventures. Memorizing involves enough complexity without having to remember what version you're in or having to constantly rethink which version you should choose.

Yes, read other translations, benefit from them, compare them, but pick your lane for memorizing and stay there. Take that decision fatigue and subsequent confusion out of the equation.

If you study with Precept, I'd suggest you go with the NASB 1995 or ESV as their studies use those versions of the Bible. If you're a Bible Study Fellowship or Community Bible Study student, go with the NIV as that is the primary text each of those organizations use.

Accept that You Can and Have Memorized

Let's take a quick test. I'm going to give you a few words, and let's see if you can complete at least some of these phrases.

—Oh, say can you see . . .

—Take me out to the . . .

—Sweet Caroline . . .

—Four score and seven . . .

—Amazing grace how . . .

—I pledge allegiance . . .

—867-53 . . .

—There's no crying in . . .

—There's no place like . . .

—Wait 'til . . . (CUB FANS ONLY!)

—Be our guest . . .

—Tale as old as time . . .

—Joyful, joyful . . .

—For God so loved the . . .

Realize it or not, admit it or not, we all memorize some things. Often music aids in the process, but not always. You can memorize. You have memorized, even if you haven't memorized Scripture.

GO DEEP STRATEGY

If You've Never Memorized the Bible, Start with Verses

Start small and start familiar. If you've never done any Bible memory before, don't start with a goal of the whole book of Romans! Start with core verses that tell about the gospel or turn your eyes toward who God is. Here are some suggestions:

John 3:16

John 14:6

Romans 3:23

Romans 6:23

Romans 5:8

Romans 8:28

Romans 8:38-39
Ephesians 2:8-9
1 John 1:9

If You Have Memorized,
Try Short Passages or Chapters

I memorized individual verses as a child. As an adult my memorization is almost exclusively passages or chapters. I find it easier to memorize this way as I study because the context gives clues to what comes next in the text. Here are a few suggestions:

Significant Chapters
Psalm 1
Psalm 23
Stanzas from Psalm 119
Matthew 6
Romans 8
Philippians 2
Hebrews 11

Short Books
Galatians
Ephesians
Philippians
Colossians
Titus
1 Peter

GO DEEP STRATEGY
Deciding What to Memorize

With 1,189 chapters made up of 31,102 verses in the Bible, the decision of what to memorize can be daunting. Just looking at those numbers can cause decision paralysis. I find that memorizing in conjunction with a Bible study or following along with a sermon series can provide excellent pacing.

If your pastor is preaching through a book of the Bible verse by verse (I know that is rare these days), you may want to memorize a portion of the text he's preaching on each week. If you're participating in a Bible study, instead of just filling in the blanks, memorize the text. Trust me when I say that if you memorize the text, filling in the blanks will be as easy as falling off a log!

GO DEEP STRATEGY
Remember, Before Anything Else, the Purpose

Full disclosure: as I've mentioned I first started memorizing because I was taught to as a child with positive reinforcement. My parents literally set me up for success with this by introducing it early and rewarding the behavior. Along the way, I learned to memorize for prizes thanks to AWANA and other ways churches incentivise memory work in children. I was good at it, I was competitive, and if there was something to be won, I'd win it. I'm not proud of this, by the way, but God's Word does not return void, even when we put it in under less than holy circumstances.

As adults, we rarely find ourselves in situations where we're competing for a chocolate bar or trophy when it comes to memorizing, but it's still important for us to connect with the purpose of it. We've already seen evidence from the psalmist that he treasured God's Word in his heart so that he would not sin against God.

As you read God's Word widely, you will come across other Scripture that will point to related purposes. Here are a few to think on:

- Jesus, when being tempted by the devil in the wilderness, does not simply resist, but resists by quoting Scripture. If Jesus depends on Scripture, how much more must I? Take a look.

Matthew 4:1-11

1 Then Jesus was led up by the Spirit into the wilderness to be tempted by the devil.

2 And after He had fasted forty days and forty nights, He then became hungry.

3 And the tempter came and said to Him, "If You are the Son of God, command that these stones become bread."

4 But He answered and said, "It is written, 'MAN SHALL NOT LIVE ON BREAD ALONE, BUT ON EVERY WORD THAT PROCEEDS OUT OF THE MOUTH OF GOD.' "

5 Then the devil took Him into the holy city and had Him stand on the pinnacle of the temple,

6 and said to Him, "If You are the Son of God, throw Yourself down; for it is written, 'HE WILL COMMAND HIS ANGELS CONCERNING YOU'; and 'ON their HANDS THEY WILL BEAR YOU UP, SO THAT YOU WILL NOT STRIKE YOUR FOOT AGAINST A STONE.' "

7 Jesus said to him, "ON THE OTHER HAND, IT IS WRITTEN, 'YOU SHALL NOT PUT THE LORD YOUR GOD TO THE TEST.' "

8 Again, the devil took Him to a very high mountain and showed Him all the kingdoms of the world and their glory;

9 and he said to Him, "All these things I will give You, if You fall down and worship me."

10 Then Jesus said to him, "Go, Satan! For it is written, 'YOU SHALL WORSHIP THE LORD YOUR GOD, AND SERVE HIM ONLY.' "

11 Then the devil left Him; and behold, angels came and began to minister to Him.

Furthermore, did you know that of Jesus' words recorded in the New Testament, approximately 10% are quotations from the Old Testament? That'll preach.

- Paul, who also quotes extensively from the Old Testament, continually reminds his readers to take care where they set their minds and to renew their minds. A key way we can do this, though certainly not the only way, is through memorizing Scripture. Consider these Pauline excerpts with my boldface added:

Colossians 3:2

2   **Set your mind** *on the things above, not on the things that are on earth.*

Philippians 4:8

8   *Finally, brethren, whatever is true, whatever is honorable, whatever is right, whatever is pure, whatever is lovely, whatever is of good repute, if there is any excellence and if anything worthy of praise,* **dwell on** *these things.*

Romans 8:5-8

5   *For those who are according to the flesh* **set their minds** *on the things of the flesh, but those who are according to the Spirit, the things of the Spirit.*

6   *For the mind set on the flesh is death, but* **the mind set** *on the Spirit is life and peace,*

7   *because the mind set on the flesh is hostile toward God; for it does not subject itself to the law of God, for it is not even able to do so,*

8   *and those who are in the flesh cannot please God.*

Romans 12:1-2

1   *Therefore I urge you, brethren, by the mercies of God, to present your bodies a living and holy sacrifice, acceptable to God, which is your spiritual service of worship.*

2   *And do not be conformed to this world, but be transformed by* **the renewing of your mind,** *so that you may prove what the will of God is, that which is good and acceptable and perfect.*

2 Peter 3:1-2

1   *This is now, beloved, the second letter I am writing to you in which I am stirring up your sincere mind by way of* **reminder,**

2   *that you should* **remember** *the words spoken beforehand by the holy prophets and the commandment of the Lord and Savior* spoken *by your apostles.*

What we think about matters. Where we set our minds is critical.

GO DEEP STRATEGY

The Through-Storyline Exhortation to "Remember"

You can dodge "memorize," but you can't dodge "remember." Throughout both the Old and New Testaments, God's people are told to remember and often given specific ways to remember including Passover, stones at Gilgal, and countless others. Watch for commandments to "remember" and "not forget" as you read God's Word widely.

GO DEEP STRATEGY

Recite to Someone

I know, this sounds like a terrible idea! Who wants to recite what they're memorizing? Only the theater majors among us, I think. While our goal will not be to "perform," the act of reciting out loud to another person helps the memorization process.

Your listener will be able to identify errors immediately to keep you from reinforcing mistakes, prompt you as needed, and be able to give both feedback for improvement as well as encouragement along the way. Knowing that you will be reciting brings focus to the memorization process that can be lacking when you're being your own boss.

It is uncomfortable at first, but becomes easier over time. Seriously, and it works!

GO DEEP STRATEGY
Write It Out

Writing the verse or verses that you're memorizing can be a game-changer. Writing. Long hand. Not typing. I tend to use this strategy early on in the process so I can visualize the words and because science shows that handwriting information increases our ability to remember. Typing is faster, but handwriting is stickier![9]

GO DEEP STRATEGY
Think It Through

Children often memorize by rote. They repeat sounds and words without even thinking about meaning. As a child I had a long-standing feud with my parents over a particular television commercial with a phrase that included the words, "Tragedy tomorrow, comedy tonight." I heard "Skagedy" and I fought for it to the end. "Skagedy tomorrow, comedy tonight" made no sense. What even is "skagedy"? It is nothing. It is a child learning by rote and mishearing the word "tragedy." Clearly there was no thought in my memorization. "Skagedy" it was for me! Have I mentioned how patient my parents have always been?

As adults, we have more tools in our belts than simply "hear and repeat." While retaining random facts becomes more difficult as we age, we grow in our ability to handle information and hold it together by understanding meaning. We can move from one word to the next, from one sentence or verse to the next because we can reason through the train of thought.

Using inductive questions and keen observation can help us follow the logic of a passage in order to remember it more easily even as our memory horsepower decreases and our hard drive fills. Let's take the Mem stanza of Psalm 119 as an example.

---

9. Stack Overflow. Why writing by hand is still the best way to retain information. https://stackoverflow. blog/2022/11/23/why-writing-by-hand-is-still-the-best-way-to-retain-information/

Psalm 119:97-104

97 *O how I love Your law!*
    It is my meditation all the day.
98 *Your commandments make me wiser than my enemies,*
    For they are ever mine.
99 *I have more insight than all my teachers,*
    For Your testimonies are my meditation.
100 *I understand more than the aged,*
    Because I have observed Your precepts.

101 *I have restrained my feet from every evil way,*
    That I may keep Your word.
102 *I have not turned aside from Your ordinances,*
    For You Yourself have taught me.
103 *How sweet are Your words to my taste!*
    Yes, sweeter than honey to my mouth!
104 *From Your precepts I get understanding;*
    Therefore I hate every false way.

KEY WORDS

Word. After reading Psalm 119 and marking references to the Word of God, I notice that of the seven English synonyms (eight in Hebrew) for *the word* that are used in Psalm 119, the psalmist here makes use of only five of them and repeats "precepts" and "word." This may seem nit-picky, but the synonyms in Psalm 119 can become very slippery, so by giving myself some toeholds in the text, I at least know where the odds will be in my favor.

Meditation. Although it only occurs twice in the stanza, meditation lies at the heart of the psalmist's behavior. It is why he is wiser, has more insight, and understands more than those around him. As I read, I note there are three categories of people he outpaces because of his "all the day" meditation: enemies, teachers, and the aged.

More than. A little more covert in the text is the concept of "more than" that makes memorization easier for a Hebrew speaker. Even in English, however, we see this pattern in:

- wiser than, v. 98
- more insight than, v. 99
- more than, v. 100
- sweeter than, v. 103

BEGINNING AND END

As the stanza opens, I key in on the English alliteration of "love your law." I also notice that while the stanza opens with the psalmist *loving* God's law, it closes with him *hating* every false way. Reasoning then, I can remember that the one who loves God's law will hate every false way.

FIRST HALF / SECOND HALF

As I slow down and look closely at the material, I also notice that the first half of the stanza presents positive benefits for the psalmist based on his meditation on and observation of God's Word, while the second half of the stanza focuses more on the negative, in a sense—the way the Word restrains or holds the psalmist back from evil.

KEY BENEFITS

I'm reminded that meditating on God's Word offers clear and tangible benefits. It makes the psalmist:

- wiser than his enemies, v. 98
- more insightful than all of his teachers, v. 99
- full of more understanding that the aged, v. 100

Why meditate? It gives the psalmist, and by implication any who would follow his example, a wisdom leg up on those around him who might otherwise be the better bet. This wisdom also restrains the psalmist from every evil way (vv. 101, 104).

WATCH FOR PATTERNS

The longer I sit with a passage the more patterns I see, the more hooks in the text help me to remember and move forward through the text. If you have some time, why not sit with this passage for a bit on your own and see what other patterns you notice that I may have overlooked. What you discover and see for yourself, you will remember better than if someone simply tells you what to see!

GO DEEP STRATEGY

Use Mnemonics Early

Mnemonics are memory devices to help people remember. They are often based on patterns, acronyms, or word associations. I view mnemonics as temporary braces for the memorization building process. They help me stay oriented in the text as I build the permanent structure and often fall away when the real work is done. I use them as bread crumbs along the path until I *know* the path for myself.

Looking back at how I've worked through Psalm 119:97-104, you'll see how I've noted some general mnemonics that are content based that I will likely remember over time. Sometimes, though, I'll come up with simple patterns to remember in the short term. For Psalm 119, it is very easy to confuse which synonym is used for the Word of God in each line, so in this stanza a simple mnemonic for me is to use the sequence of how they occur:

Line 1	**L**aw
Line 2	**C**ommandment
Line 3	**T**estimony
Line 4	**P**recept
Line 5	**W**ord
Line 6	**O**rdinance
Line 7	**W**ord
Line 8	**P**recept

A simple glance at this reminds me that of the eight synonyms for God's Word, *precept* and *word* occur twice. When I divide the psalm into two sections, precept ends both the first and second section. I also see "WOW" reading down in lines 5 through 8 which will remind me that synonyms will occur in the sequence of word, ordinance, word. This likely seems cumbersome, but when scaffolding the passage and encoding it, you'll be amazed at how every little memory aid will help.

Before you dismiss this, let me do a quick parlor trick for you. When I was in the eighth grade, I devised a mnemonic for a literature test to remember ten common literary devices. The test was on a Friday in September 1979. Here's my mnemonic: I do seem sort of scared for Friday in September.

I	Irony
Do	Dialogue
Seem	Simile
Sort	Sarcasm
Of	Onomatopoeia
Scared	Symbolism
For	Foreshadowing
Friday	Flashback
In	Imagery
September	Satire

Yes, I did have to Google a bit to fill in a couple of the "s" entries, but for a 40-plus-year-old mnemonic, I think it held up pretty well.

GO DEEP STRATEGY

Listen, Listen, Listen

Early in my memorizing journey I used a microcassette recorder to help me memorize passages. I'd read the passage several times trying to place emphasis on the same words and syllables each time so I could listen to the passage on repeat. Today, I use the Bible Memory app which allows me to play the same passage on loop for up to ten repetitions! It's a miracle!

Inductive Bible Study Will Propel Memorization

In recent years, I've begun to think of inductive Bible study and memorization as fraternal twins. They bear a striking resemblance to one another in their focus on slowing down and considering the text.

Memorizing Scripture as an adult forces me into the inductive process because I need to actively think through the *Who, What, When, Where, Why,* and *How* questions in order to remember content. When I see key words, I immediately recognize and latch onto them as places to grip the text as I move from one verse or phrase to the next. Comparisons and contrasts, terms of conclusion, and thematic elements also help me remember content. I'm always on the look out for any distinctive in the text that will help me to remember. I'm pretty sure that I took to inductive study so quickly because I've naturally done it for years as I've memorized Scripture.

If you study the Bible inductively but haven't done any intentional memorization, you'll likely find that memorizing comes relatively easy to you if you give it a try because the process sets the text in your head and your heart. Have you ever heard Kay Arthur rattle off columns of Scripture as she's speaking? I believe it is largely because she reads the Bible out loud and studies inductively—both powerful ways to help you remember God's Word!

DRAW NEAR THIS WEEK

Pick one or more of the opportunities for drawing near. Feel free to continue with what you have been reading or try a new book.

- Start or continue reading the Gospel of John to help you begin building the habit of daily fixing your eyes on Jesus.
- Start reading in 1 Samuel if you're already a pro in Genesis. Keep reading in increments of at least 30 minutes as you're building your reading habit.
- Start reading in Genesis if you've never read it before.
- Pick one or two of the following shorter epistles to read in one sitting: Galatians, Ephesians, Philippians, or Colossians.
- Get a bookmark and start reading in the Psalms. This book will take almost five hours to read, so I suggest reading it concurrently with other books so you don't get overwhelmed or feel stuck.
- Get another bookmark and continue reading Proverbs. Again, I suggest you read this along with something else so it doesn't feel too repetitive.
- Choose a verse(s) to memorize and write it/them below.

- Choose a passage you'd like to memorize and write it, word for word, below.

DISCUSS TOGETHER

These questions can be used in a discussion group if you're using this book in a Bible study setting or book club. You can also use them to process through what you're learning on your own.

- Where have you been reading in the Word this week?
  - How has it been going?
  - What have been your biggest takeaways?
  - What are you specifically applying in your life?
  - What questions have you had that may need further study?
- What new strategies have you been trying this week?
  - What has worked?
  - What strategies are you thinking about trying this week?
- Has memorizing Bible verses been part of your spiritual growth journey?
  - If so, what prompted it?
  - How do you go about memorizing?
  - How has it affected your thinking and life?
  - Have you picked a specific translation that you use for memorizing? If so, which is it?
- Is memorizing something that you're willing to try now? Why / why not?
- Is there a verse or passage you've been thinking about memorizing?
- What concerns do you need to bring to the Lord this week with regard to His Word? What other concerns do you need to bring to Him?

READ TOGETHER

If you're meeting with a group, spend some of your time reading the Bible aloud. This week take turns reading some of these passages that you may want to consider memorizing: **Psalm 1, Psalm 23, Psalm 100, Matthew 6, Romans 8, Philippians 2,** and **Hebrews 11**. As always, remember that reading aloud is for those who want to participate and listening is completely acceptable! When you're finished reading, spend some time praying for one another.

CHAPTER 8

The Why and How of Going Together

Encouraging One Another in the Word

THE FIERCE INDIVIDUALISM OF AMERICAN CULTURE, and much of western culture, makes us susceptible to a particular strategy of the adversary that goes all the way back to the Garden. Historically, we Americans at least take pride in pulling ourselves up by our own bootstraps, wanting things our way, and being fiercely independent. The dogged responsibility in this type of world view goes a long way toward building a strong country, but leaves an exposed Achilles' heel.

Let's take a moment to revisit Genesis 3, noting specifically how sin causes the man to react to the presence of God.

Genesis 3:1-10

1 Now the serpent was more crafty than any beast of the field which the Lord God had made. And he said to the woman, "Indeed, has God said, 'You shall not eat from any tree of the garden'?"

2   The woman said to the serpent, "From the fruit of the trees of the garden we may eat;

3   but from the fruit of the tree which is in the middle of the garden, God has said, 'You shall not eat from it or touch it, or you will die.' "

4   The serpent said to the woman, "You surely will not die!

5   "For God knows that in the day you eat from it your eyes will be opened, and you will be like God, knowing good and evil."

6   When the woman saw that the tree was good for food, and that it was a delight to the eyes, and that the tree was desirable to make one wise, she took from its fruit and ate; and she gave also to her husband with her, and he ate.

7   Then the eyes of both of them were opened, and they knew that they were naked; and they sewed fig leaves together and made themselves loin coverings.

8   They heard the sound of the LORD God walking in the garden in the cool of the day, and the man and his wife hid themselves from the presence of the LORD God among the trees of the garden.

9   Then the LORD God called to the man, and said to him, "Where are you?"

10   He said, "I heard the sound of You in the garden, and I was afraid because I was naked; so I hid myself."

We could spend hours exploring the truths in Genesis 3. We could look at the way the serpent questioned what God had said. We could follow the path of deception from entertaining a question about the goodness of God to finally taking and eating the fruit. This passage overflows with life-changing truth. In this moment, though, let's focus simply on the man and the LORD God. Prior to eating the fruit, what characterized the relationship between God and the humans? What changed after the man and his wife ate the fruit?

Sin brought separation and ultimately death. Instead of dwelling in the presence of God, the man and his wife hid from God and were ultimately cast out of the Garden because of their sin. The serpent persuaded them to break relationship with God which brought with it brokenness of every other kind.

The adversary is in the business of separation. It's one of his core competencies. God created man in His own image to be in relationship with Him and with one another. Sin breaks that. In a sense you might say that what God brings together, the adversary seeks to blow apart. We see it first recorded in Genesis, and we see it played out every day. Think just of the divorce culture that we live in. It's but one example of a division epidemic.

So what does this have to do with Bible reading? More than most people imagine. Again, back to modern individualistic society. In literate cultures today where people have access to their own Bibles, people for the most part try to go it alone in reading the Bible. Is solitude and personal time with the Lord important? Of course it is. But when we try to go it alone in life, we are asking for trouble, particularly when we try to go it alone in areas of utmost importance.

Consider the words of Solomon:

Ecclesiastes 4:9-12

9 *Two are better than one because they have a good return for their labor.*

10 *For if either of them falls, the one will lift up his companion. But woe to the one who falls when there is not another to lift him up.*

11 *Furthermore, if two lie down together they keep warm, but how can one be warm alone?*

12 *And if one can overpower him who is alone, two can resist him. A cord of three strands is not quickly torn apart.*

As I am rewriting this book, I am not doing it alone. The journey is too long and left to myself and my own doubts, I will surely give up before it is done. You are reading this today because of a group of ministry partners who have met with me week by week to give feedback and encouragement in the process, to pick me up when I've fallen down, to encourage me to keep taking steps forward. I'm able write because I do not do it in isolation.

I believe one of the adversary's most potent lies today that he whispers in the ears of believers is this: "You are a terrible Christian! You should be able to follow Jesus all by yourself and you can't. You are awful!" The truth of the matter, though, is that we are not on our own to follow Jesus. He has both given us His Spirit and has given us one another—other people in whom His Spirit also dwells. Before we move into some practical ways to walk together, consider these encouragements from Scripture:

John 14:16-20

16 "I will ask the Father, and He will give you another Helper, that He may be with you forever;

17 that *is* the Spirit of truth, whom the world cannot receive, because it does not see Him or know Him, but *you know* Him because He abides with you and will be in you.

18 "I will not leave you as orphans; I will come to you.

19 "After a little while the world will no longer see Me, but *you* will see Me; because I live, you will live also.

20 "In that day you will know that I am in My Father, and you in Me, and I in you.

Hebrews 3:13

13 But encourage one another day after day, as long as it is still *called* "Today," so that none of you will be hardened by the deceitfulness of sin.

Hebrews 10:23-25

23 *Let us hold fast the confession of our hope without waver-*
    ing, for He who promised is faithful;

24 *and let us consider how to stimulate one another to love*
    and good deeds,

25 *not forsaking our own assembling together, as is the habit*
    of some, but encouraging one another; and all the more as
    you see the day drawing near.

Throughout the New Testament we're reminded that Christians are part of a body. We are part of each other. While Jesus does tell us not to "practice righteousness" in front of people—not to pray and give and fast for show—to shut our door and pray to our Father who is in secret, we are still to encourage one another. As Paul clearly teaches in 1 Corinthians 12, we are one body with many members each of whom needs each other.

TIPS AND STRATEGIES FOR GOING TOGETHER

Here are some simple ways to start going "together" in God's Word!

GO TOGETHER STRATEGY
Find a Paul

What, you ask, is a "Paul"? A *Paul* is a person who is more spiritually mature than you are, who can disciple you in the faith and help you along in your spiritual growth and understanding of Scripture by modeling what a walk with Jesus looks like. You don't need someone who is perfect—good thing since nobody makes the cut—just someone who has a mature and growing faith.

A Paul will help you learn how to "accurately handle the word of truth" (2 Timothy 2:15) and encourage you to keep on keeping on, to stay in the Word, and to apply what you're learning.

This kind of mentor will be able to encourage you when the going gets tough—and it will get tough at times because we are in a war. Jesus

Himself warns, "In this world you will have tribulation" (John 16:33). A good mentor will remind you that the verse does not stop there, but continues with "but take courage, I have overcome the world."

Read in Front of the Kids

For a big part of the population, caring for children (especially small children) is an easy excuse for not reading the Bible. Who would fault them, really? Little ones—be they children or grandchildren—seem omnipresent. Toddlers are everywhere all the time. If you have little people in your life, you probably know that it doesn't matter how early you get up in the morning, because the littles will wake up ten minutes later. Some of you understand this totally. Those who have never lived with children may not. Those of us whose children are grown and gone sometime experience repression in this area, having forgotten how grueling the preschool years can be!

> *If you have little people in your life, you probably know that it doesn't matter how early you get up in the morning, because the littles will wake up ten minutes later.*

You may be at a place in life where you can sit quietly and read the Bible almost anytime day or night. I was there two weeks ago. Then we bought a puppy and I'm reminded of the days of small children. I was still learning to read the Bible in the midst of the chaos of two talkative children (one who on a couple of occasions fell asleep mid-sentence and awoke the next morning finishing said sentence), an old, talkative Dalmatian, and a couple of Great Dane puppies. Reading environments change as our lives change. Some times will be easier and others far more challenging. It is critical to pursue God through His Word during all of them.

Some of us have life circumstances that make it easier to pursue actual "quiet" with God. Others have circumstances, which are often blessings, that make it more difficult to find quiet. I prefer to read in the dead quiet, but during loud seasons of life I learned to adapt. I learned to read with children's videos in the background, with boys running through the house yelling, and with a dog announcing every single car approaching on our street.

At times during the season, I found God would wake me up earlier and earlier so I could have some quiet time with Him. Other times I'd stay up past midnight just to find the quiet and eventually fall asleep drooling on my Bible—but more than anything, I learned to bloom where I was planted and in the presence of those planted around me.

A funny thing happened to me as I started reading the Bible more and more in front of my kids instead of trying to cloister myself off to do it alone. They wanted to join in with me. At one point, I was reading through my Bible on my laptop—before Logos Bible Software! As I read, I marked key words and phrases with different colors and symbols. My then nine-year old, Brad, thought this was cool beyond belief! Who would have known? Of course, whatever the older one did, the younger one had to do too (garnering her the nickname "R2 Me2"). So as I'd point to the words on the screen that needed to be marked, Katie would click the mouse and giggle. Don't for a moment think that I'm going to tell you that I read with the same comprehension when I was being "helped." I didn't, but I did gain more than if I hadn't read at all.

The bigger benefit here, though, was letting my kids see how important the Bible was to me and giving them the opportunity to experience the fun in Bible study. Sure, pointing and clicking was mainly at familiar words, but they began associating the Bible with something enjoyable. My son even picked out "joy" as a key word in Philippians. Who'd have thought? As I'd read, I was able to explain some of what I was reading to them, not out of a devotional or a storybook, but directly out of God's Word, which is where we all want our kids to be someday . . . directly in the Word of God for themselves.

Read to the Kids

Yup. Read to your kids or grandkids from your Bible, simplifying the tough words as you go. Read to them from children's Bibles, let them watch the Bible on video . . . do whatever it takes and whatever you can to introduce them to the Word of God. Make it a family affair! Sometimes that may have to serve as your Bible time for the day, but when they understand how important the Bible is, they'll probably be more understanding when you want to take some time to read the Bible for yourself. No promises, but give it a try, and always remember your responsibility to teach what you are learning to the next generation—be it your kids or your grandkids. Remember the words from Deuteronomy that we looked at earlier!

Deuteronomy 6:4-7

4   *"Hear, O Israel! The L*ORD *is our God, the L*ORD *is one!*

5   *"You shall love the L*ORD *your God with all your heart and with all your soul and with all your might.*

6   *"These words, which I am commanding you today, shall be on your heart.*

7   *"You shall teach them diligently to your sons and shall talk of them when you sit in your house and when you walk by the way and when you lie down and when you rise up.*

If you can't "justify" the time you personally spend reading the Bible, you can justify it for them. You need to know for yourself what you are charged to pass on.

GO TOGETHER STRATEGY

Learn to Ask a Simple Question: "Where are you reading in the Word?"

Learning to ask this question and inviting others to ask it of me has been life-changing. I've found that if I'm asked this question at least once a week, I will stay in the Word; not perfectly, but regularly. Knowing that someone is going to ask is enough to keep me honest. The connection with another person or people in fellowship around the Word at regular intervals helps to keep me on track better than when I try to go it alone.

Looking back on my life, this has been a regular part of my spiritual rhythms though it has looked slightly different from season to season. Let me tell you about a couple of those seasons here.

ONE-ON-ONE READING

In my early 20s, my husband and I volunteered as youth leaders in our local church. The youth pastor's wife, Kar, and I hit it off right away. We both studied the Bible in college, Kar at Moody Bible Institute in Chicago and me at Wheaton, and we liked talking all things biblical. One day as we were chatting, we decided we should read part of the Bible, take her kids to the park, and chat about what we'd read. We set a date and time about a week out and I asked Kar, "What do you want to read?" Her answer: "Genesis." Okay, six days to read Genesis, no problem! Let's go. And so we read and met and talked and talked and talked. At the end she said, "We should do this again." I said, "Great, when and what do you want to read?" I'll bet you can guess her answer. "Same time next week. Let's read Exodus." And so I was introduced to the concept of running with the runners.

When you commit to set aside time to discuss your reading with another person, it affects your resolve and helps you move forward. I learned from Kar not to be afraid of suggesting a faster and more vigorous pace with certain people. I would never have had the guts to suggest Genesis in one week, but she did and I was happy to match her pace.

Not everyone in the world is Kar, but if you're looking to grow, ask God to bring a person along who can be a pacesetter in your life.

When you commit to set aside time to discuss your reading with another person, it affects your resolve and helps you move forward.

CASUAL READING GROUPS

Kar and I met on our own for quite a while, simply reading and discussing. Eventually, though, we invited others. Instead of everyone reading the same material, we'd meet for an hour once a week with the simple query: *Where have you been in the Word this week and what have you been learning?* At times we met over our lunch hours, other times we'd meet during the "off" service at church. Today, with Zoom, the ability to get together is simpler than ever.

GO TOGETHER STRATEGY
Encourage Others in the Word

In our information-saturated world, many people veer from the simplicity of the Word of God toward well-meaning, but lesser-than devotional material. I want to be careful here, because devotional books can encourage people and if the choice is a devotional book featuring a verse of Scripture or no Scripture intake at all, I'd have to admit that typically some is better than none. Still, forever seared in my memory is a summer small group as a high school youth leader where we asked the girls to share where they had been reading in their Bibles during their quiet times. In a group of well over 20 girls, each one told about what they had read not in their Bibles, but in their devotional books. My heart broke and an even greater zeal started growing in me to help people read God's Word for themselves. Don't settle for middlemen who tell you what they think God is saying in His Word. Be like the psalmist and declare, "I have not turned aside from Your ordinances for You Yourself have taught me!" (Psalm 119:102).

Get Involved in a Bible Study

The simplest way to start going together in the Word is to find a Bible study at a local church. Be discerning as you choose; pick a class that actually studies the Bible and not just what people think about the Bible. Many churches offer study options as "Bible Studies" that would be better termed devotional book studies. Understand that I'm not saying that book clubs or studies are wrong, just that the words of people cannot replace or substitute for the Word of God.

I've spent most of my adult life writing inductive Bible studies, pointing people not to my words but helping them handle God's Word for themselves. People often thank me for this as though it is something I do simply to help other people. It is not. Yes, I know that writing studies does help other people; yes, I know God has gifted me to do this to build up the body (1 Corinthians 12); but at the end of the day, writing Bible studies keeps me in the Word of God. Studying to teach or write provides me accountability with teeth.

Walk Together Day By Day

During the COVID-19 shutdown of early 2020, my dear friend Elizabeth tired of the isolation that Illinois imposed on its citizens and decided to use Zoom to fight back with a simple solution for community. Each morning she invited friends from church to join her on Zoom for something she called "God Time Together." She simply opened a Zoom room and spent about 15 minutes chatting with friends from church and then asked each person where they were going to be reading in the Word. Then everyone shut off their mics and turned their cameras off for the next 30 minutes to spend time with the Lord in the Word. At the end of the 30 minutes, she'd call everyone back and debrief for the next 15 minutes or so letting people share what they had seen during their time in the Word.

I became involved with the morning time during March 2020 and decided to share it with others later that year, inviting others from outside our local church to a 50-day time in the Word called IGNITE. Four years later, we've seen God change lives through the combination of regular time in the Word and diligent accountability.

IGNITE is a 50-day high-accountability small group that I run several times each year via Zoom that helps people gain traction in their Bible reading and learn how to walk together. For more information on future sessions, visit pamgillaspie.com/ignite.

Get Accountable

Have you ever had an exercise buddy? I used to run before dawn with a friend back when I thought I would eventually learn to like running. Turns out I love to exercise if there is a ball involved, but running never quite worked for me. It took me years to discover this, though. I kept running and didn't miss days because I had a running partner and great conversation. Even though the pillow called, I'd roll out of bed in the morning to meet my friend Cress at the YMCA to run together. It's one thing to roll over and go back to sleep if you're planning to run on your own, it's another if someone is waiting for you in the snow at the Y.

Accountability in the Word works with the same principle. You show up because you've committed and any potential sloth will not only affect you but your accountability partner, too. Don't underestimate the power of a friend. Proverbs puts it this way, "Iron sharpens iron, so one man sharpens another," Proverbs 27:17.

Commit to a Set Time Frame

Counterintuitive though it may be, think about setting a start and end time to your accountability with an understanding that you'll reevaluate when your commitment comes to the end. Many of us hesitate to enter into commitments at all because we fear that we'll get in over our heads or we're afraid of backing out and leaving other people hanging.

Establishing start and end times and providing on- and off-ramps help us get started more easily and focus more diligently. Most of us can entertain the thought of finding an accountability group for 30, 50, or 90 days much more easily than we can bear the thought of making an indefinite commitment that we fear might last forever. Start small and build.

GO TOGETHER STRATEGY

Try Reading Aloud Together

One of the most powerful ways to jump-start your time in the Word is to read the Word aloud with others! If you've never done it before, realize that I understand it sounds, well, odd. We are not a culture that is accustomed to the public reading of much of anything. In the biblical book of Nehemiah, though, we see the public reading of the Word of God! Nehemiah's account takes place after the Babylonian captivity when some of the people begin to return to the land of Judah. As you read, note who's there, how they listen, and how long the reading takes.

Nehemiah 8:1-8

1   *And all the people gathered as one man at the square which was in front of the Water Gate, and they asked Ezra the scribe to bring the book of the law of Moses which the Lord had given to Israel.*

2   *Then Ezra the priest brought the law before the assembly of men, women and all who could listen with understanding, on the first day of the seventh month.*

3   *He read from it before the square which was in front of the Water Gate from early morning until midday, in the presence of men and women, those who could understand; and all the people were attentive to the book of the law.*

4   *Ezra the scribe stood at a wooden podium which they had made for the purpose. And beside him stood Mattithiah, Shema, Anaiah, Uriah, Hilkiah, and Maaseiah on his right*

> *hand; and Pedaiah, Mishael, Malchijah, Hashum, Hashbad-*
> *danah, Zechariah and Meshullam on his left hand.*
> 5 *Ezra opened the book in the sight of all the people for he*
> *was standing above all the people; and when he opened it,*
> *all the people stood up.*
> 6 *Then Ezra blessed the Lord the great God. And all the*
> *people answered, "Amen, Amen!" while lifting up their*
> *hands; then they bowed low and worshiped the Lord with*
> *their faces to the ground.*
> 7 *Also Jeshua, Bani, Sherebiah, Jamin, Akkub, Shabbethai,*
> *Hodiah, Maaseiah, Kelita, Azariah, Jozabad, Hanan,*
> *Pelaiah, the Levites, explained the law to the people while*
> *the people remained in their place.*
> 8 *They read from the book, from the law of God, translating*
> *to give the sense so that they understood the reading.*

Over the course of the past several years, I've been hosting Bible reading retreats where we spend Friday night, all day Saturday, and Sunday morning reading the Word of God aloud in small groups, each person taking a chapter and reading it aloud while others follow along in their own texts.

I was introduced to the idea by some godly women at my church growing up—Jan Brooks and Jean Schrek. They hosted weekends where they would read a harmony of the Gospels and then the rest of the New Testament in a weekend. While I was never able to attend one of those, I saw the changed lives that resulted from women seeing the Word of God in all its glory!

My weekend reads follow on the same premise of reading the Word aloud chapter by chapter, but instead of using a harmony of the Gospels we work our way through various books of the Bible in different combinations. We always read at least one Gospel account, we always mix both Old and New Testaments, and I try to work in at least one book that is hard to read on your own. The way I figure, if it's too hard to read Leviticus on your own, why not let a friend help hoist you over the hill!

It is impossible to explain to you the power of the Word read in community, so let me simply offer a few testimonials.

WHAT OTHERS ARE SAYING ABOUT READING GOD'S WORD IN COMMUNITY

"Man does not live by bread alone, but by every word that comes from the mouth of God."

Reading retreats are the "Thanksgiving meal" of my walk with God. I "eat" everyday, but I feast at the retreat. Retreats are not cluttered by words of men (e.g., sermons, teachings, commentaries), but intentionally serve only the rich, sweet Word of God. I leave filled with a renewed closeness to my Savior and can't wait to return next year.

————

Have you ever found something you didn't know you were looking for? Or had a prayer answered that you didn't even know you had? This is what I love most about our God! He intercedes where we may not even see the need. I grew up religious, thinking I knew God. I wasn't looking for something I thought I already had. Through a succession of life circumstances including my mother's suicide, a verbally abusive relationship, and struggling children, God brought me to the Bible and to the One True God who left His Word for us to read and His Spirit to bring all truth to our remembrance. It seems that life can run a similar pattern to the cycle of abuse where tension builds, there's some sort of incident, things are reconciled or resolved followed by a period of calm. I used to be tossed about by life's struggles as explained in James 1:6, but since reading the Word daily I am no longer coming to God only in the incident or chaos of life and then trailing off when life is calm.

———

I believe Jesus when He told the Pharisees in Matthew 22:29 that they do err not knowing the Scriptures and the power of God. God's Word is life to us and I praise God for transforming my mind as in Romans 12:2 and causing my soul to thirst for Him like David did in the parched and weary land of Psalm 63. I say open your Bibles and read ... "For the word of God is living and active, sharper than any two-edged sword, piercing to the division of soul, and of spirit, of joints and of marrow, and discerning the thoughts and intentions of the heart." (Hebrews 4:12, ESV).

———

The Bible reading retreat for me was a peaceful escape from the busyness of everyday life. It allowed me to immerse myself in God's Word, surrounded by others savoring the joy of turning each page of God's amazing story. With no distractions, the retreat allowed for uninter-rupted hours of reading, providing a much-needed respite for the mind and nourishment for the soul. The time away being in God's Word provided the perfect opportunity to recharge, gain new perspectives, and find hope once again.

———

While I have long loved reading God's Word aloud with others, I only recently attended my first Bible reading retreat. The women there with me were delightful and insightful, and reading Scripture and discussing it with them was like finding a refreshing spring together and drinking it in. Since the retreat, I have endeavored to read more Scripture aloud and I'm loving it! I am excited to attend another Bible reading retreat in the future.

178

If you're interested in hosting your own Bible Reading retreat, check out Appendix 3 in the back of this book.

GO TOGETHER STRATEGY
Another Way to Read Aloud Together

One of my favorite Bible reading stories from my years in ministry is of three friends of mine who decided to read the whole Bible out loud together over the course of about a year. All had little kids at the time, so they hired a babysitter to hang with their children and they spent every Monday morning at McDonald's reading chapter by chapter through the entire Bible. Not only did they grow together in the faith, but they had interesting conversations along the way with other patrons who wanted to know what they were doing!

GO TOGETHER STRATEGY
Enlist Someone to Pray for You

Don't underestimate the power of prayer. Ask God for what you need and when others ask "How can I pray for you?" . . . tell them.

If no one asks you, who can you ask to pray for you? Ask those you're reading with. Ask a mentor. Ask your small group. If no one comes to mind, ask God to cross your path with someone who will pray with you and for you!

GO TOGETHER STRATEGY
Ask for Advice

Don't be shy in asking others for advice. Chances are you know people who are serious students of God's Word. Ask them what has worked for them and what hasn't. Learn from the people that God places around you. This isn't a sign of weakness, it's a sign of smarts. Why stumble forward when we can stand on the shoulders of others and learn from both their successes and failures?

179

Grow Up Together!

If it's too hard to read the Bible on your own, stop trying to do it by yourself. God put us in community so that we would grow up together! Listen to Paul's words in Ephesians 4.

Ephesians 4:11-16

11 And He gave some as *apostles, and some as prophets, and some* as *evangelists, and some as pastors and teachers,*

12 *for the equipping of the saints for the work of service, to the building up of the body of Christ;*

13 *until we all attain to the unity of the faith, and of the knowledge of the Son of God, to a mature man, to the measure of the stature which belongs to the fullness of Christ.*

14 *As a result, we are no longer to be children, tossed here and there by waves and carried about by every wind of doctrine, by the trickery of men, by craftiness in deceitful scheming;*

15 *but speaking the truth in love, we are to grow up in all aspects into Him who is the head,* even *Christ,*

16 *from whom the whole body, being fitted and held together by what every joint supplies, according to the proper working of each individual part, causes the growth of the body for the building up of itself in love.*

Stop trying to go it alone! Let's go deep and wide in the Word together!

DRAW NEAR THIS WEEK

Pick one or more of the opportunities for drawing near. Feel free to continue with what you have been reading or try a new book.

- Start or continue reading the Gospel of John to help you begin building the habit of daily fixing your eyes on Jesus.
- Start reading in 1 Samuel if you're already a pro in Genesis. Remember to read in increments of at least 30 minutes as you're building your reading habit.
- Start reading in Genesis if you've never read it before.
- Pick one or two of the following shorter epistles to read in one sitting: Galatians, Ephesians, Philippians, or Colossians.
- Get a bookmark and start reading in the Psalms. This book will take almost five hours to read, so I suggest reading it concurrently with other books so you don't get overwhelmed or feel stuck.
- Get another bookmark and start reading through the book of Proverbs concurrently with another book.
- Ask a friend to be your reading buddy for the next 30 days. If you're in a class, this should be easy!

DISCUSS TOGETHER

These questions can be used in a discussion group if you're using this book in a Bible study setting or book club. You can also use them to process through what you're learning on your own.

- Where have you been reading in the Word this week?
  - How has it been going?
  - What have been your biggest takeaways?
  - What are you specifically applying in your life?
  - What questions have you had that may need further study?
- What new strategies have you been trying this week?
  - What has worked?
  - What strategies are you thinking about trying this week?
- Who has been most influential in your life in encouraging you in the Word?
  - What did that person do?
- Have you ever had a reading buddy or someone who helped you stay on track with your reading?
  - If so, how did it go?
  - If not, is it something you'd be interested in trying? Why / why not?
- Have you ever had the opportunity to read God's Word aloud in community?
  - If so, what were the circumstances?
  - What did you gain from it?
- What are some ways you could be intentional about going together with others in God's Word and encouraging others in the Word?
- What concerns do you need to bring to the Lord this week with regard to His Word? What other concerns do you need to bring to Him?

READ TOGETHER

If you're meeting with a group, spend some of your time reading the Bible aloud. This week take turns reading through the four chapters of **2 Timothy**. These words were written by Paul to Timothy, his son in the faith, just prior to his death at the hands of Rome. It is a book of challenge and encouragement. As always, remember that reading aloud is for those who want to participate. Those who prefer to listen are always welcome to follow along as others in the group read. When you're finished reading, spend some time praying for one another.

CHAPTER 9

Help When You're Stalled or Stuck

Gaining Traction and Moving Forward

THERE IS NOT JUST ONE WAY TO GROW IN GOD'S WORD, but going deep in the Word, reading widely in His Word, and going together is one combination that regularly leads to sustainable growth. Still, even with a solid sustainable plan, we can find ourselves stuck from time to time, lacking the traction we need to continue moving forward.

So let's take some time to consider a few more simple strategies to help in going either deep or wide in the Word when you feel stalled, stuck, or worse!

TIPS AND STRATEGIES FOR WHEN YOU'RE STUCK

Pray, Pray, Pray

We've talked about this before, but don't forget to pray. When I started reading the Word, I had finally realized that I couldn't power my own success in Bible reading even though I had a BA in the stuff and loved to read. I knew from 1 John that God gives us what we ask for when it is in accordance with His will, and I knew that me in His Word was His will. And so I prayed from 1 John 5.

1 John 5:14-15

14 *This is the confidence which we have before Him, that, if we ask anything according to His will, He hears us.*

15 *And if we know that He hears us in whatever we ask, we know that we have the requests which we have asked from Him.*

Based on these verses, I came to God in prayer and asked Him for the desire to read His Word and the practical wisdom to figure out how.

You know what? He answered. Don't try and gut it out on your own. Don't pretend that you're good and righteous and able. Submit and ask God to do in you what you cannot do in yourself. Then act like He is going to answer and watch Him work.

Stop Preparing and Get Started

I like planning things to do, but sometimes the actual doing of them is tougher. Right now, you are preparing to start because you're reading this book. I hope this book propels you forward. Please don't get stuck here. Don't spend your Bible-reading time making a schedule or reading commentaries about the Bible. Don't waste your time reading footnotes or general inspirational works. Read the Bible. Jump in and read. Pray and move forward. As I've already mentioned, commentaries can help and devotionals can encourage, but they need to be in addition to God's Word, not in place of it. They should be read-after texts, not before. If you want life change, stick with the God-breathed Word.

GAIN TRACTION STRATEGY
Remember It's Not Rocket Science

God put the Bible in the language of common people. The New Testament was not written in high style classical Greek, but in Koine Greek, the common Greek language of the day. Jesus' boys learned the Torah, the first five books of the Old Testament. The Word was and is accessible. The Bible was never intended to be a coffee table book that just sits around looking good or a shelf book that you have "just because every house needs one."

The Bible is not rocket science! We like to believe it is because in some way we feel that excuses us from the responsibility to know it and live by it. If we can't understand it, we reason, how could God ever hold us accountable for what is in it? But it is not rocket science. It is within our grasp. We need desperately to accept that fact and bring that truth to others.

GAIN TRACTION STRATEGY
No Quotas

Whatever you do, don't set a chapter per day quota. Okay, I know that most people will pull out a calculator to do the math, so let me save you the time. To make it through the Bible in a year, you'll need to average about three chapters a day. However, please, please, please don't lock into a strict three chapters a day expectation or you'll miss the flow and risk turning a beautiful relationship into an assignment.

Read logical portions. Stop at the end of an epistle, read through the conclusion of a story. Don't stop because you've "done your time." I think back to when my son was in the second grade. Each day he had to read for thirty minutes. At the outset, it didn't matter if he was mid-sentence when the timer went off, HE WAS FINISHED. Reading was a chore, and all he wanted was to be done!

One day, however, he asked if he could read a joke book for his reading time. I told him that he could read the back of a ketchup bottle if he wanted to, he just had to read! This revolutionized his reading time! Since then, he has learned to enjoy reading (well, some of the time).

GAIN TRACTION STRATEGY
Change Your Default

We all have a default. What happens in your life when nothing in particular is happening? What do you do when you have a spare moment or some unexpected free time? Most people today when given a free moment begin to engage their phone in some way whether it is doom scrolling on social media, checking email, watching videos or something else. We move toward something to fill gaps. When I first started Bible reading, my default was *Sports Illustrated;* now I often default to email.

If you're stuck or having trouble gaining traction in your reading, identify and change your default. Instead of defaulting to music in your car, try defaulting to your audio Bible. Instead of blindly plunking down in front of Hulu, swap out for your Bible instead. It takes some repetitions to become accustomed to a new default position, but you can change your "factory settings."

GAIN TRACTION STRATEGY
Set the Timer

While I'm typically not a watch-the-clock kind of girl with Bible reading, sometimes setting a timer can break inertia—and not only in Bible reading. If you can't seem to move, just set the time for a few minutes and start. Maybe you'll set it for seven or ten or fifteen, just to overcome the immobility. When your timer goes off, you'll likely have enough momentum to keep reading.

GAIN TRACTION STRATEGY
Relax

Enjoy the Word! Be diligent, yes; but don't be uptight. Don't succumb to guilt and try to "make up" days. Find a comfortable spot to sit, put your feet up, and learn to enjoy spending time with your God. View your time in His Word as a time of rest and restoration. If reading through the Bible in a year is too fast for you, then find out what pace works for you and walk that pace.

GAIN TRACTION STRATEGY
Read Your Physical Bible Along With an Audio Bible

Reading along with an audio Bible can help you stay engaged with the text as it keeps going even when your mind is tempted to wander off. Both your eyes and ears will be involved in the process. You won't be tempted to stop because you can't pronounce a name—the narrator will keep on going!

GAIN TRACTION STRATEGY
Make Appointments

There are stages and seasons in life when pursuing time with God becomes incredibly difficult. When we are too busy to breathe, we may need to make "appointments" with God. Just as you would block time on the calendar for a dear friend, schedule time when you can meet uninterrupted with God. Ink it on the calendar and don't schedule over it. During times of crisis, when you feel soul-starved for God, be aware when He takes the initiative. I've had times of intense busyness when I've been crying out to God for time to meet with Him; times when I've felt a deep need to sit quietly in His presence but have had screaming toddlers and other responsibilities from which I simply could not divest myself.

I've found at times like these when I've been seeking time with God that I'm often awakened in the middle of the night or very early in the morning—really awakened. The first time this happened, I went for about three nights running, waking up and being annoyed before I finally suspected that God was answering my prayer for time alone with Him. Although I had been thinking more along the lines of my husband taking the kids for the day, God apparently had another way of providing the quiet time that I needed. Like Samuel, though, I didn't quite "get" the first message.

GAIN TRACTION STRATEGY
Wake Up, Get Up

Since those first middle of the night wake-ups, I'm more aware that when my soul is craving quiet but my life is loud and crowded, God has an uncanny knack of waking me a little before five o'clock in the morning. When this happens, my natural tendency is to roll over and go back to sleep, but I find that is usually the wrong choice for me. Particularly when I'm having a hard time getting into the Word, I find the principle of "Wake Up, Get Up" to be helpful. If God wakes you up, get up and meet with Him. Similarly, when the house quiets at night and you find yourself unduly awake, I promise you'll find more wisdom in the Word of God than you ever will on any streaming service.

GAIN TRACTION STRATEGY
Look to the Goal, Not the Obstacles

Why do we spend so much more time looking at the obstacles instead of focusing on the goal? So often we obsess; *It's too hard! It's too long! I don't have the time!* Stop it and shift. Look to the goal of Jesus. When a runner competes in a race, he fixes his eyes on the goal. When the obstacles distract, resist the temptation to meditate on them and instead fix your eyes on Jesus as the author of Hebrews exhorts.

GAIN TRACTION STRATEGY
Remember That It's a Relationship

We've talked about this a bit, but the importance bears repeating. How do your relationships hold up when you ignore them? Sure, there are some relationships that you can put on hold occasionally that don't suffer, but just think what life would be like if you went through the day ignoring your spouse, your son, or your daughter. Even the dog gets bent out of shape if she doesn't get her fair share of time.

Why do we think we can maintain an intimate relationship with our God if we do not invest time with Him? In fact, a relationship with God should be the primary relationship in our lives. It's the one that provides the glue for all the others. I have the power to love my husband in a much greater fashion and with more capacity when God is my first love. Second place to God is far higher than first place without Him.

GAIN TRACTION STRATEGY
Ice Cream and the Chicago Cubs

I'm a die-hard Cubs fan. If you don't live in Chicago, you can't fully understand. Anyway, a treat in our house during the middle of the summer when the kids were growing up was to stay up late when the Cubbies played on the West Coast, eating ice cream and watching baseball while ignoring bedtimes.

Katie, who was four years old at the time we started this tradition, turned into a huge baseball fan over the summer. She absolutely loved the Cubs—or so I thought! As we made our way into autumn and the Cubs were at home for October (as they were for nearly all of the 1990s) I came to realize that she didn't love my Cubs, she loved her ice cream! We had a Pavlovian response going on. Ice Cream . . . Baseball . . . Ice Cream . . . Baseball. Stick with me here.

If you really hate to read, why not set up a Pavlovian response of your own? Sit in your favorite chair with your favorite treat if that's what it takes to overcome your inertia. Who's to say you can't set up a system

191

of Bible . . . Ice Cream . . . Bible . . . Ice Cream. Associate your reading with something you enjoy if reading itself is not yet enjoyable to you. Shallow? Probably, but I'm not above shallow pragmatism!

GAIN TRACTION STRATEGY
Remember That Some Is Better Than None

Some of us fall into the cognitive disorder of all-or-nothing thinking. The idea is "If I can't do it perfectly, I won't do it at all." Don't fall for this lie. Just like a bad workout is better than no workout at all, so also some time in the Word is better than none!

TIPS AND STRATEGIES TO KEEP MOVING

Even when we're not actively fighting inertia, we can learn new practices to keep us engaged and propel us forward in our current reading as well as to prepare us to carry on in less-than-optimal circumstances.

MOVE FORWARD STRATEGY
Go on a Personal Retreat

Years ago on a retreat for the adult leaders of our church's high school ministry, our youth pastor had an interesting afternoon planned for all of his volunteer staff. He sent us out on our own for two hours with only our Bibles, a pen, and some paper. The instructions: spend time with God out in the field, the woods, anywhere on the camp property where we could be alone. Leaving the meeting area, the faces told the story. Some in the group were thrilled. Others stunned—"Two hours? What on earth am I going to do for two hours alone with just my Bible?!"

At the end of the weekend, however, person after person shared how the two hours flew by, how they were unexpectedly the highlight of the weekend by far! You may be thinking, "Well, this must not have been a very fun group." Quite the contrary. We were 20-somethings who had worked together for several years and had great fun playing together on these leadership retreats, and yet when it came down to it, the two hours of solitude made space for God to break into lives in very significant ways.

Taking solitude a step further, you may want to go away for a weekend in the Word. You don't need fancy accommodations, just simple sleeping quarters and a quiet place away from life's normal distractions to focus on God and His Word. You don't need guided activities or anyone to lead you. Just bring your Bible, a journal, a pencil, and ask the Spirit of God to guide you through His Word.

MOVE FORWARD STRATEGY
Carve Out Time for a Mini-Retreat

At certain life stages, the thought of a weekend or even an all-day retreat may seem too difficult. If you have little kids or are caring for an elderly relative, a weekend may not be possible right now. That doesn't mean you can't find some time, even if it's more limited. Maybe you could trade childcare duties with a friend so each of you has a little time on your own while the other watches the kids. Perhaps instead of going away for a weekend, you can find a quiet park where you can read outside for a couple of hours. Think about it. Pray about it. See what God does.

MOVE FORWARD STRATEGY
Learn Quiet

Some of us may need to learn how to embrace quiet in a culture that tries to fill every moment with sound and distraction. Many of us have screens and speakers in every room of the house, not even counting the ones that stalk us in our computer bags and pockets. Even in places designed for quiet, like libraries, we now pop the buds into our ears and push the sound directly in.

Those earbuds, though, can be a help in learning quiet. If you have a hard time concentrating because of ambient noise or commotion, you may want to consider a brown noise generator to help you concentrate. It works for me! Most of us are familiar with the white noise produced by television or radio static. It can block other noises but is abrasive to many ears. Apps and YouTube channels now provide noises in other "colors." I like brown noise because it is a lower frequency and helps me to focus.

MOVE FORWARD STRATEGY
Learn to Block Noise

If you have little kids running around, it's probably best not to block all ambient noise. Sometimes we need to learn to block noise by practicing. It's not easy, but you can learn. As I'm rewriting this paragraph, I'm sitting in a quiet and peaceful house with an old dog on the couch. When I first wrote it, however, this paragraph went down with *The Wild Thornberrys* playing in the background.

When I was in high school my boyfriend at the time, now husband, was the sound engineer for a Christian rock band. I spent the better part of a summer sitting in a sound studio with guitars and drums blaring—and I mean blaring—reading *Gone with the Wind*. Sure it was tough at first, but I learned to focus on the text and ignore the background sound, loud as it was.

MOVE FORWARD STRATEGY
Build Habits

When I first wrote about Bible reading over 20 years ago, I did not have established habits. I read voraciously, but because I had children, my reading flexed. I read nearly every day, but the times varied like snowflakes. I told myself during this season that it would get better as I got older and it has, but it has been due to accountability more than anything, of having the time and resolve to walk with others every morning on Zoom.

There are times when life will force us into a flexible Bible reading mode. If you're there, keep reading and keep praying for the desire.

When my Bible reading time of day varied, the biggest problem I faced was that it was too easy for God to be pushed out by end-of-day fatigue. Being a night owl, I have often used the late night quiet to both read and write, but sometimes when the sun sets, I've simply had all the life and energy sucked out of me.

A good friend and mentor of mine who reads at a set time of day explains that she would no sooner leave the house in the morning without having spent time with God than she would leave the house without taking a shower, brushing her teeth, or combing her hair. Over the years, my movement has been more in this direction toward an early-to-bed, early-to-rise mentality.

Maybe this concept will connect with you, especially if you're the I-can't-leave-the-house-without-my-makeup type. Personally, if I'm clean and have a baseball cap, I'll go just about anywhere if push comes to shove—except, of course, when I'm in the South—which obviously demonstrates my issues with routine. Even with my flexibility mindset, God has been moving me toward more set times with Him now that my kids are grown and on their own.

MOVE FORWARD STRATEGY
Don't Get Too Academic

As I've mentioned, one of the main reasons I dislike Bible reading schedules is that they move the reading into the academic realm. Remember here that I love the academic realm! I'm a student at heart, always have been. We encounter problems, though, when we become singularly academic with the Bible and begin to divorce it from application. Knowledge and study without prayer and application puffs up. So study and learn for sure, but never without praying and applying or you risk puffing up with dead doctrine instead of humbly submitting to the living Word.

Treat Yourself!

Rewards. I know, we're back into shallow, pragmatic, and potentially unspiritual territory, but hear me out. A little incentive can make me move, because rewards are fun! It works for kids and it's worked for me as an adult in different arenas, too. Years ago after the birth of my second baby, I held on to several extra pounds and I was not alone. Three of my friends were also struggling to lose post-baby weight. Instead of struggling and suffering alone, we set up a little accountability group and contest. First one to drop ten pounds would win a pot of about $50. Now, it wasn't that much money—even then—but just the game of it, the potential reward, kept a bunch of chocolate out of my mouth. It kept me drinking water, it kept me exercising, and it kept me tracking my intake. Eventually it won me $50, because rewards can be fun!

I'm encouraging rewards because they work, but did you realize that the concept is also entirely biblical? Clearly we don't work our way to heaven and we don't look to temporal things as spiritual rewards—although people twist the Word of God to say both of these often. Still, throughout both the Old and New Testaments of the Bible, we find God talking about rewards. As early as Genesis 15:1 God tells Abram, "Do not be afraid, I am a shield to you, your very great reward" (NIV). Later in one of the most famous of biblical chapters, Hebrews 11 (sometimes referred to as the "Faith" chapter or "Hall of Faith"), we read that the one who comes to God must believe "that He is and *that* He is a rewarder of those who seek Him."

We see, too, in Hebrews 11:6 that Moses followed God and gave up the passing pleasures of Egypt because he was looking to the reward. God is a rewarder. You'll see this as you read both deep and wide. It's not works salvation, because no one can work his way to God, but God is a rewarder. It's there in black and white.

So set a reward for finishing, and make it worth attaining. How about a leisurely weekend away or maybe a shopping excursion for something special? Be sure to make the treat something that you want, and don't let yourself have it until you do the job!

MOVE FORWARD STRATEGY

Checkpoints and Mini Rewards

The only thing that works better than big rewards are little rewards along the way! So why not give yourself some little treats when you make progress in your Bible reading? It doesn't need to be anything big, just enough to keep you motivated and moving.

Maybe you'll treat yourself to dinner out with a friend. Maybe it will be a new pair of shoes. It could be as simple as a mocha with whip! Who knows, maybe it will even be that great Greek-based, hard-back commentary on Hebrews at your local seminary bookstore that you couldn't break down and spend the $39.95 on before! Okay, or maybe not . . . whatever works for you. Just make it fun! Now, will you have to treat yourself for the rest of your life to keep you reading the Bible? Hopefully not. This is just one of those ways to train yourself and make it fun to build the habit of being in God's Word.

Make sure that you have treats set up for finishing these books: Leviticus, Numbers, each of the big prophets (Isaiah, Jeremiah, Ezekiel), 1 Chronicles, and Revelation.

Revelation is a surprisingly quick read, but many people avoid it out of fear, and 1 Chronicles has a steep start because of the genealogies at the start of the book.

Accept Grace

As I've mentioned, I'm a recovering perfectionist. I hate messing up. I hate falling short. I dislike mistakes in others, but I despise them in myself. It pains me to my bones to fall short of a goal that I've set. The goals that I've set in my perfectionism over the years have been way too high. Perhaps you relate. When I don't perform to my unrealistically high expectations, my natural tendency is to beat myself up. Now, I may outperform others, but that for me is not enough if I know I have not done my best. I can accept imperfection in others (well, usually), but learning to accept it in myself has been tough even though I am fraught with imperfections.

So when you mess up and miss reading for a day or a week or longer, admit that you are human, ask God's forgiveness and help, and get back on the horse. Don't dwell on the mistakes and failures. Accept forgiveness and grace, look forward, bask in the love that God lavishes on you, and move toward Him.

Our tendency when we aren't performing as we think we should is to shrink back and hide, to stop trying and to drift—at least that's how it goes with me. This is exactly what the adversary wants . . . for us to float through life, not making any waves at all. Instead, when we're not on top of our game, we need to draw near to God, knowing that He not only loves us now, but that He loved us when we were enemies (Romans 5:10). We need to accept that we are saved by grace *and* that we grow and are sanctified by grace (Galatians 3:3). We can never be good enough on our own. It is all God!

Jesus Every Day

One of my favorite theology professors in college advised our class that no matter where we were reading in our Bibles that we should meet with Jesus in the Gospels for at least some time every day. His suggestion was to read even a few sentences from the Gospels each day to help in keeping our eyes fixed on Jesus. Do I always do this? No. I can tell you, though, when the world is beating me down, the place I run to in the Word are the Gospel accounts because there is nothing like looking on the face of Jesus to quicken my spirit!

MOVE FORWARD STRATEGY
Experiment to Find Your Sweet Spot

As you're learning to read and study your Bible, experiment a bit. Try reading at different times of the day. Try studying in different parts of the house. Read while you eat—I have an embarrassing number of Bibles with pizza stains. Read in a chair, read in bed, read at the kitchen table. Read on your computer or tablet, read out of your regular Bible. Memorize.

I can give you pointers, other people can give you tips, but in the end, you'll have to discover what rhythms and strategies work for you, and you won't figure those out without jumping in and trying some different approaches. Have fun!

MOVE FORWARD STRATEGY
Do What Works

Go with what works for you. My husband built his Bible reading habit at Caribou Coffee. Not going to lie, it was an expensive way to build the habit but it was the best investment of money that we've ever made. The third-space ambient noise and a spot outside of the house worked amazingly for him as he built the habit. He can read anywhere now, but those Caribou years were critical for him.

Some people need early morning, others flourish with late night. Our stage of life often affects the when and where of reading. Be aware of this, figure out what is most effective, and do what works for your current life stage. "Nothing works for me" is not an option. Some approaches will work better than others. Stick with the experimentation until you find your style and keep going!

Keep Moving

Don't underestimate the importance of momentum and don't ignore the power of inertia. If you realize you can't make it through the Bible in a year—or meet whatever your goal is—so what? Reassess your end goal and keep moving. There's nothing magical about reading through the Bible in a year, but it is important to keep going and keep making progress.

When you're sitting still, it's hard to get moving. Physics tells us that a body in motion tends to stay in motion. The same thing is true with reading habits. Once you get moving, it's much easier to stay moving than to start, stop, and start again. Even if you have to move slowly, keep moving. Remember that some reading is better than no reading at all.

Accept Your Weaknesses

You are human. I am fallen. That's okay. Jesus loves fallen human beings so much that He died for the whole lot of us. If you're thinking that you probably can't pull the Bible-reading thing off by yourself, you're right! Even if we do plow through some of the words just by our own grit and tenacity, we will never understand it without the Spirit's work in our lives. With God's power at work within us, we can make it through His Word. If we depend on ourselves, we will almost certainly fail. The beauty here is that the Bible tells us that God's power is perfected in our weakness (2 Corinthians 12:9). And that is where we need to focus—on the power that is at work within us, not on our own frailties and weaknesses!

MOVE FORWARD STRATEGY
Remember the Power at Work in You

In other words, don't even think about puffing up when you start making progress. The book of Proverbs counsels that "Pride *goes* before destruction, and a haughty spirit before stumbling" (Proverbs 16:18). As we make progress in reading through the Word, God will use it to change us from the inside out, to conform us to look more and more like Jesus.

The sin nature, however, still rears its head and tries to persuade us that we have made spiritual progress because of our own hard work, tenacity, and downright superior skills. Baloney! It is by the grace of God that we are saved, and it is by the grace of God that we are sanctified and now have the power to persevere. Remember, once you've started thinking how good you are, you've taken your eyes off the goal, off of Jesus, and you're headed for trouble.

MOVE FORWARD STRATEGY
Don't Be Surprised by Opposition

The adversary doesn't want you reading the Bible. It's that simple. Cut off from the Word of God, you are spiritually impotent. Do nothing and you are of no real concern to the enemy of your soul; you're actually playing for his team. Immerse yourself in the Word of God and you become an armed soldier. Does this mean we should let a sleeping dog lie, so to speak, and stay away from the Word? In the words of Paul, may it never be!

Do realize that while the difficulty for us in reading the Word may seem like it is mainly in issues of time or worldly things, the battles we fight in life are truly of a spiritual nature. In Ephesians 6:12, Paul tells us "our struggle is not against flesh and blood, but against the rulers, against the powers, against the world forces of this darkness, against the spiritual *forces* of wickedness in the heavenly *places*." It is for this reason that he goes on to tell us to arm ourselves with the full armor of God.

A friend of mine recounts a time when she first started teaching Bible studies and had such a bad day that she came close to cancelling her evening class before she realized that she was likely facing spiritual opposition to the class, so she pushed through and held the class.

Our son contracted chicken pox just prior to being able to receive the vaccine and on the eve of my husband and I leading a group of young adults to the Urbana Missions Conference. It may have been the result simply of living in a fallen world, but to this day I think it was spiritual opposition to the trip. After much prayer, Brad stayed with Grandma and Grandpa and we went to a life-changing Urbana conference.

When opposition comes, remember our God is bigger!

MOVE FORWARD STRATEGY
Put on the Full Armor of God

Truth be told, when you start swinging the sword of the Spirit, it becomes evident to all that you are part of the active battle. The Word is the one offensive weapon we have on the battlefield (although it, too, is used defensively at times). Paul tells us about the equipment that we need to deal with as soldiers on this spiritual battlefield.

Ephesians 6:13-17

13 *Therefore, take up the full armor of God, so that you will be able to resist in the evil day, and having done everything, to stand firm.*

14 *Stand firm therefore,* HAVING GIRDED YOUR LOINS WITH TRUTH, *and* HAVING PUT ON THE BREASTPLATE OF RIGHTEOUSNESS,

15 *and having shod* YOUR FEET WITH THE PREPARATION OF THE GOSPEL OF PEACE;

16 *in addition to all, taking up the shield of faith with which you will be able to extinguish all the flaming arrows of the evil one.*

17 *And take* THE HELMET OF SALVATION, *and the sword of the Spirit, which is the word of God.*

Although all analogies fall short, think for a moment of an American football game. Eleven players from each side stand between the lines at any given point. More guys are members of the team but spend a majority of the game riding the bench or roaming the sidelines. They've dressed the part, but as long as they're outside the lines, they're not engaged in the battle. No one's hitting the guy on the bench.

Here's the point: offense draws opposition and as followers of Jesus, we're the offense. When you play offense, you need to be wearing your defensive gear. A running back would never think of carrying the ball without first putting on his helmet. Neither should you.

MOVE FORWARD STRATEGY

Move Forward Based on Faith, Not Feelings

I speak here to myself as much as anyone. Women especially need to hear this. We are creatures of feelings. This is fine in many areas of life—go ahead and enjoy the occasional chick flick. When we address issues of faith, however, we can't let ourselves run on feelings or the adversary will deceive us every time. He is far more powerful than you are on your own. No comparison.

He is the father of lies, and the schemes he uses he uses on our minds. If he can use your feelings to deceive you—and he can—he most certainly will! He doesn't fight fair. He is the ultimate liar. That is why you need and I need to know truth. We need to know the full counsel of God's Word and we need to walk by the Spirit if we are to stand a chance. Because you know what? Your adversary knows the Word of God and he will twist it at will to suit his purpose in deceiving you every time you let him.

Let's try this one on for size: Have you ever feared that you've committed the unpardonable sin that Jesus talks about, blasphemy against the Holy Spirit, or that you are the man of Hebrews 6, the one of whom the writer says, "...it is impossible to renew them again to repentance"? You don't have to be a Bible teacher (or a parent, for that matter!) very long before one of these issues pops up. It's a common scheme of the adversary to try to make believers doubt their salvation. (Just for the record, biblical scholars overwhelming agree that if you're afraid you've committed one of these sins, you haven't because if you could and had, you wouldn't care!) These verses can be terrifying if taken out of context. Whenever I have a scared student on my hands, I send them to the book of John, specifically chapter ten, which clearly teaches that of all that the Father has given to the Son, He will lose none. If this isn't assurance, I don't know what is!

Still, there are times we will not "feel" saved. We will be under attack. Guess what? If you're under attack, it is an evidence of the reality of the spiritual world. Our job? We are to stand firm in the faith (see 1 Peter 5:9). God has not given us a spirit of fear, but one of power, and of love, and of a sound mind (see 2 Timothy 1:7). He has given us weapons of warfare according to Ephesians 6, which includes both defensive weapons and the offensive weapon that is the sword of the Spirit—the Word of God.

MOVE FORWARD STRATEGY

Decide Beforehand What You'll Do When You Want to Stop

You need to understand up front that while reading the whole Bible is within your grasp, it will not be easy sailing the whole way. There will be days when you want to stop. On some days you'll feel distant from God. You may know why. You may not. You may be bored or tired or angry or frustrated or depressed. Decide in advance that when those feelings emerge, you'll seek God anyhow!

Go to the Gospels, look at your Savior, and press on diligently as the author of Hebrews exhorts. When you most feel like pulling away, press into God instead. Draw near to the throne of grace. The author of Hebrews puts it eloquently, explaining that in Jesus we have a merciful high priest who can sympathize with us because He became one of us:

Hebrews 4:15-16

15 *For we do not have a high priest who cannot sympathize with our weaknesses, but One who has been tempted in all things as we are, yet without sin.*

16 *Therefore let us draw near with confidence to the throne of grace, so that we may receive mercy and find grace to help in time of need.*

MOVE FORWARD STRATEGY

Pursue God Especially When You Feel Most Distant and Least Worthy

Ever make a big mistake? We all have and do. Maybe it was a moral failure. Maybe your mouth got the better of you . . . and then did again. Maybe a bitterness is trying to take root. Maybe you're in a mood and you're not even sure why. Ever just feel distant? Whatever the case, when we fail God like when we fail people, our first instinct is to avoid and hide. Remember Adam and Even in Genesis? Yeah, that's us, too. We feel like we're not worthy, because without Jesus we aren't! God knows our failures and He knows our frame. Jesus understands our trials and temptations. He can sympathize and He can save. We need desperately to learn the four main exhortations of the book of Hebrews (boldface in text mine):

CONSIDER JESUS

Hebrews 3:1

1 *Therefore, holy brethren, partakers of a heavenly calling, **consider Jesus,** the Apostle and High Priest of our confession;*

HOLD FAST

Hebrews 3:6

6 *but Christ was faithful as a Son over His house—whose house we are, if we **hold fast** our confidence and the boast of our hope firm until the end.*

205

Hebrews 3:14

14 For we have become partakers of Christ, if we **hold fast**
the beginning of our assurance firm until the end,

DRAW NEAR

Hebrews 4:16

16 Therefore let us **draw near** with confidence to the throne
of grace, so that we may receive mercy and find grace to
help in time of need.

PRESS ON

Hebrews 6:1

1 Therefore leaving the elementary teaching about the
Christ, let us **press on** to maturity, not laying again a foun-
dation of repentance from dead works and of faith toward
God,

MOVE FORWARD STRATEGY

Pray Some More!

Keep praying. Keep praying for the continued desire to read. Keep praying that God will open your eyes as you read to give you eyes that see
and ears that hear. Pray every time you read. Prayer is key, and yet it can
be so easy to forget, especially if you're succeeding. When we gain traction in God's Word it can be easy to forget what a gift it all is. Salvation
is a gift; the faith to believe is a gift; the desire to read is also a gift. None
of it is of you or of me. It is all of Him. Certainly, we respond, but we
need always to remember the source and to continue diligently in prayer
as we grow.

Remember that God Looks for
Whole Hearts to Support

As we come to the close of the tips and strategies for getting into the Word, let me leave you with some of the most encouraging words in the Bible that are buried in one of the less-read books, 2 Chronicles.

2 Chronicles 16:9a

> *"For the eyes of the LORD move to and fro throughout the earth that He may strongly support those whose heart is completely His."*

God is looking for people to strongly support! Ask Him for a whole heart and be encouraged!

DRAW NEAR THIS WEEK

Pick one or more of the opportunities for drawing near. Feel free to continue with what you have been reading or try a new book.

- Start or continue reading the Gospel of John to help you begin building the habit of daily fixing your eyes on Jesus.
- Start or continue reading in 1 Samuel or Genesis. Keep reading in increments of at least 30 minutes as you're building your habit.
- Pick one or two of the following shorter epistles to read in one sitting: Galatians, Ephesians, Philippians, or Colossians.
- Get a bookmark and start reading in the Psalms. This book will take almost five hours to read, so I suggest reading it concurrently with other books so you don't get overwhelmed or feel stuck.
- Get another bookmark and start reading through the book of Proverbs concurrently with another book.
- Pick a book of your choosing this week. If you've felt challenged by longer selections in previous weeks, pick a shorter book. If you're looking for something harder, mix it up and give a longer book a try. Jot down which book you've selected and why.

DISCUSS TOGETHER

These questions can be used in a discussion group if you're using this book in a Bible study setting or book club. You can also use them to process through what you're learning on your own.

- Where have you been reading in the Word this week?
- Why did you select what you selected?
  - How has it been going?
  - What have been your biggest takeaways?
  - What are you specifically applying in your life?
  - What questions have you had that may need further study?
- What new strategies for getting unstuck or maintaining momentum have you tried this week?
  - What has worked?
  - What strategies are you thinking about trying this week?
- What are your plans for reading widely when you finish this book?
  - Do you have a completion goal in mind?
  - Have you picked a reward for yourself?
- What plans do you have for studying deeply as you go forward?
  - Is there a study at your church you can join?
  - Will you take the initiative to lead a study?
- What plans do you have for going together in the Word with others?
  - Who do you have in mind to ask?
  - What, if any, challenges do you anticipate?
- What concerns do you need to bring to the Lord this week with regard to His Word? What other concerns do you need to bring to Him?

READ TOGETHER

If you're meeting with a group, spend some of your time reading the Bible aloud. This week take turns reading from the book of **Philippians**. Start at the beginning and read chapter by chapter as time allows. Always remember that reading aloud is for those who want to participate. Those who prefer to listen are always welcome to follow along as others in the group read. When you're finished reading, spend some time praying for one another.

CHAPTER 10

Go!

Readers and Hearers and Doers

WHEN I FIRST WROTE ABOUT READING THE BIBLE, I assumed that
everyone who undertook the practice with zeal would do what it said.
Call it naive, call it stupid, call it what you will, but in my youthful
optimism I never considered the pervasiveness of what I now refer to as
"Bible study malpractice."

I knew there were buttoned-down academics who got lost in the
verbs, the theoreticals, and the hypotheticals and missed Jesus. I'd read
them and I pitied them. I also knew there were those who claimed Christ
while avoiding the Word almost entirely. To a large extent, they were my
market—those who needed to taste and see the goodness of God and the
sweetness of His Word. Sometimes, though, we find ourselves in a place
where we like to hear and study the Word, but we fall off when it comes
to application.

SOME WORDS ON APPLICATION

DON'T COMMIT MALPRACTICE

Bible study malpractice happens when we know the Word and fail to align to what it says, when we fail to submit to our Lord. It happens when we can define "kindness" from the Greek yet turn and disembowel a family member with our words. It happens when we are hearers but not doers of the Word.

The goal of Bible reading and study, after all should be to know God better through His Word—and as we know Him better, to live more and more in submission to the work of His Spirit in our lives. If Bible study is making you mean, you're doing it wrong. James puts it this way:

> **If Bible study is making you mean, you're doing it wrong.**

James 1:22-25

22 *But prove yourselves doers of the word, and not merely hearers who delude themselves.*

23 *For if anyone is a hearer of the word and not a doer, he is like a man who looks at his natural face in a mirror;*

24 *for once he has looked at himself and gone away, he has immediately forgotten what kind of person he was.*

25 *But one who looks intently at the perfect law, the law of liberty, and abides by it, not having become a forgetful hearer but an effectual doer, this man will be blessed in what he does.*

How often do we think of Bible study as finishing the lesson, the workbook, or the course? Instead of filled blanks, the true measure of a successful study is what we do with what we've learned. I've realized that a bottom line approach is asking this: *Are the people who are closest to me happy that I'm reading and studying God's Word?* If you're "doing it right," they should be thrilled. The Word should be changing you day by day, moment by moment to look more like Jesus. If your people aren't thrilled that you're in the Bible, you might ask, *What am I learning that can better show Jesus?* Is God's Word changing you as you submit to the truth and apply it? It's when we start obeying that we see the life-change, the transformation! The Word should be changing you!

This doesn't mean that we'll be living in sinless perfection. We still live in a broken and fallen world and we fight sin in the flesh, but we do it by the power of the Holy Spirit as we apply what He is teaching us through the Word because we don't come for information only! We don't come to show others where they fall short. We come to God through His Word humbly asking Him to use His Word to change us. Remember Paul's words to Timothy:

2 Timothy 3:16-17

16 *All Scripture is inspired by God and profitable for teaching, for reproof, for correction, for training in righteousness;*
17 *so that the man of God may be adequate, equipped for every good work*

God's Word teaches us. It shows us where we are wrong (reproof), how to make it right (correction), and trains us in righteousness so that we will be Navy-SEAL equipped for every good work. Conversely, when we know what God's Word says and what it means but don't take the time to humbly apply it in our own lives, we commit malpractice.

DON'T STRAND THE RUNNER

As I write this paragraph, baseball season is around the corner. I'm reminded that studying God's Word without applying it is like stranding the leadoff runner on third. In baseball, when a leadoff hitter reaches third base, the hope for scoring is great! If the leadoff batter triples, the subsequent batters must bring the runner home to score. If the runner doesn't score, the triple means nothing. If the player doesn't cross home plate, everything that has been done prior is empty.

The same is true in Bible study when we don't apply what we learn. If you know what the text says and know what the text means but fail to apply it, you have stranded the runner on third base. We must finish the job by applying what we have learned in our own lives!

Let's put this in football terms, particularly for my friends in the southeast! Knowing what the text says and figuring out what the text means without applying what we've learned is like pushing the ball down the field past the opponent's 20-yard line and then fumbling for a turnover. So much progress, so much work squandered! When the ball is in the red zone, you need to come away with at least three!

LET THE HOLY SPIRIT DO HIS WORK IN YOU

Remember that as we're applying the Word, we need to let the Holy Spirit do His work in us and we need to let Him do His work in others.

A great temptation in the application department is wanting to apply God's Word to everyone else, to every social issue that we see, to our kids, our parents, our spouses, and our dogs instead of letting it do its purifying work in our own lives. Are there times we'll speak the truth in love to others? Of course. That said, when we apply the Word, we need to focus on how God wants to use it to change *us* first and foremost! Always be applying!

CHARTING THE PATH FORWARD

We've talked about going deep in God's Word, studying so we know what the text says, what it means, and how to apply it. We've discussed the benefits of also reading God's Word widely to understand the through storyline of Scripture, to gain needed context for deep study, and to simply learn to rest in and enjoy God's Word. We've considered the importance of engaging in the Word of God together, not trying to be a Lone Ranger but instead living out the reality that if we are in Christ, we are members of His body and are to grow up together to maturity. We've covered much ground, with a variety of tips, strategies, and approaches for each area.

Let's take some time to think through how you can start to integrate what you've been learning into your own rhythms of life with regard to studying and reading God's Word. I'll leave room for you to write in the book if you choose. No pressure. :)

- What's on your mind at this point?

- What Bible reading/studying approaches haven't worked for you in the past? What, if any, stories (a.k.a. lies) have you told yourself based on past failures?

- What are a few of the strategies you'd like to try going forward? How can these help set you on a new course?

- What are some ways you think your life might change if you regularly engage in God's Word?

- What do you need from God for you to be able to move forward? Take some time to ask Him for what you need.

- Who are some of the people you'd like to walk with you?

- What are specific next steps you can take today?

- What's the reward you're going to get for yourself when you complete Leviticus? Ezekiel? The whole Bible? (Again, I'm not above shallow if it's pragmatic!)

If this is too open-ended, don't worry; I'll give some suggestions for specific next steps before we're done, but sit with this for a bit. You know you better than I do, and if you're actually a follow-the-plan kind of person, you probably wouldn't be here with me to start with. We both know that, right?

ACTION STEPS FOR STARTING

If you haven't started already, it is time to get going! Hopefully you've started charting your course by thinking and praying through the questions in the previous section. If you're still unsure or need some more specific instructions, here are some first steps.

1. PRAY

We've talked about it often. Pray for God's help. Pray for the desire to read the Word, for the people to go with you, for the way of approach. As Elisabeth Elliot said in her book *Love Has a Price Tag,* "Pray when you feel like praying. Pray when you don't feel like praying. Pray until you feel like praying."

2. FIND A FRIEND AND STATE A GOAL

Goals come to life when they're shared. Unstated goals are just ideas. You can read through the Bible on your own but, just like exercise, if you have a partner, your odds of success skyrocket. Studies show that simply telling someone you have a goal increases your odds of success to 65%. Having a true accountability partner increases them to 95%. Ask God to lead you to the right reading buddy.

3. CHART A COURSE

I strongly encourage you to pick a starting point and then read God's Word book by book from there without adhering to a strict plan. Why? Because we're all here together because plans have failed us.

—PICK A STARTING POINT

As mentioned in the Read Wide section, here are three good starting points:

- Book by book starting in Genesis
- Book by book starting in 1 Samuel
- Book by book starting in any of the Gospels (Matthew, Mark, Luke, or John)

Continue to read through the Bible book by book, alternating shorter books with longer ones to keep up your momentum and tracking your progress in your table of contents as you go.

OR

—PICK A PLAN

If you're still convinced you need a plan, go ahead and find one online; there are many. No, I don't have one that I recommend because they have never worked for me.

217

4. JUMP IN

If you're ready to commit, why not start strong? Here are a couple of my favorite ways to launch!

—COFFEE SHOP JUMP-START

Take a morning and read as much as you can while drinking an extra large latte. You'll be amazed at how far you can read before noon if you can find some space without distractions! Don't forget your AirPods!

—WEEKEND READ ROCKET LAUNCH

Even better, gather some like-minded friends for a weekend read and you won't be tempted to feel behind in your reading for the rest of the year when you launch with several books in one weekend!

FOUR REMINDERS AS YOU START

WORD BEFORE WEB

Almost everyone interacts with the internet almost every single day. A simple "Word Before Web" practice will keep you in the Word daily. I'm not a tattoo girl, but if I were, I might ink this one on my swiping thumb.

RULE YOUR TOOLS

Use your pens and pencils as you study, but make sure that you're in charge! You rule your tools. Never let them rule you. When you're reading widely, be especially careful not to let your pens stop you from seeing the greater context. It's important to see the trees, but pens and pencils can keep you from seeing the forest. Rule your tools!

PROGRESS, NOT PERFECTION

You will not do this perfectly. We're aiming at continued progress over time, not perfection by tomorrow. So remember that some is better than none and keep going little by little, day by day, and watch what God will do with that over the long haul.

SIMPLE IS SUSTAINABLE

While the temptation of complex and exhaustive systems may be compelling, most of us mere mortals do better with simple. Pray for the desire for God's Word, trust that He will answer you, and then go deep, go wide, and go together in His Word!

GO!

DRAW NEAR THIS WEEK

Pick one or more of the opportunities for drawing near. Feel free to continue with what you have been reading or try a new book.

- If you didn't work through the questions on pages 215–216, start there to build a foundation for moving forward.
- Start or continue reading the Gospel of John to help you begin building the habit of daily fixing your eyes on Jesus.
- Start or continue reading in 1 Samuel or Genesis. Keep reading in increments of at least 30 minutes as you're building your habit.
- Pick one or two of the following shorter epistles to read in one sitting: Galatians, Ephesians, Philippians, or Colossians.
- Get a bookmark and start reading in the Psalms. This book will take almost five hours to read, so I suggest reading it concurrently with other books so you don't get overwhelmed or feel stuck.
- Get another bookmark and start reading through the book of Proverbs concurrently with another book.
- Pick a book of your choosing this week. If you've felt challenged by longer selections in previous weeks, pick a shorter book. If you're looking for something harder, mix it up and give a longer book a try. Jot down which book you've selected and why.

DISCUSS TOGETHER

These questions can be used in a discussion group if you're using this book in a Bible study setting or book club. You can also use them to process through what you're learning on your own.

- What's on your mind at this point? What has been your key takeaway from our time together?
- What do you think of the concept of Bible study malpractice? Have you seen this as a problem in your life? If so, how?
- What, if any, stories (a.k.a. lies) have you told yourself based on past failures? What truths can you use to replace those?
- What are a few strategies you'll keep going forward? How can these help set you on a new course?
- What are some ways you think your life might change if you regularly engage in God's Word? Have you started seeing any changes yet?
- Who are some people you'd like to walk with you?
- What are specific next steps you can take today?
- What's the reward you're going to get for yourself when you complete Leviticus? Ezekiel? The whole Bible?
- Where have you been reading in the Word this week?
  - What have been your biggest takeaways?
- What book of the Bible do you plan on reading next? Why?
- What plans do you have for studying deeply as you go forward?
- What plans do you have for going together in the Word with others?
- What do you need from God for you to be able to move forward? How will you ask Him to help you?

READ TOGETHER

If you're meeting with a group, spend some of your time reading the Bible aloud. This week take turns reading from the book of **James**. Start at the beginning and read chapter by chapter, paying particular attention to what he says about being doers of the Word. Again, remember that reading aloud is for those who want to participate. Others can join in through listening. When you're finished reading, spend some time praying for one another.

APPENDIX 1

5-Minute Guide to the Old Testament

In the beginning **God** creates. **Adam** is the first man created, **Eve** the first woman. God creates them without sin and places them in the Garden of Eden. The serpent (later identified as Satan), however, quickly deceives them. Eve eats the forbidden fruit (from the tree of the knowledge of good and evil) first and gives it to her husband, Adam. Through this act of sin death enters the world and God banishes Adam and Eve from their beautiful garden home.

Although man rebels against God, God immediately predicts the coming of a Savior who will crush the head of the serpent (Messianic Covenant). Jesus eventually fulfills this prophecy, but in the meantime sin and death rule the day.

Eve bears Adam many children, the first two being **Cain and Abel**. Cain, resentful when God rejects his offering and accepts his brother Abel's, murders Abel. Sin gains speed and man continues downhill until God has simply had enough.

Saying He regrets making man, God tells **Noah** to build an ark in which he and his family will be saved from the coming destruction—a worldwide flood. Noah obeys and God saves him, his wife, his three sons, and their wives. After the Flood, God places a rainbow in the sky as a sign of His covenant with all living creatures that He will never again destroy the entire earth by water.

Noah's sons, Japheth, Shem, and Ham, become fathers of all the nations. Over time the population of the world increases and people again veer off course. In pride they determine to build a tower reaching to heaven but during the construction God confuses their languages and thwarts their plans.

Abraham, originally named Abram, is the first major character on the scene after the Flood. Abram and his wife, Sarai (whose name later changed to Sarah), live in the land of Ur. God tells Abram to leave his land and go to another one He will show him. Abram trusts God and packs his bags, taking his wife and household with him. Although God changes his name to Abraham and promises to make him a great nation, Abraham is within view of being triple-digit old with no blood-related heir in sight.

What he does have, though, is a get 'er-done wife. After waiting "long enough" Sarah decides to act. She gives her handmaiden Hagar to Abraham as a second wife to scoot God's promise along. Not a good idea. Hagar bears Abraham a son named Ishmael but Sarah resents the outcome. Ironically the son of Sarah's plan is not the son of God's promise. He will be born later to Sarah.

Isaac is God's fulfilled promise to Abraham. Like his father, Isaac possesses a promise of descendants but has no children for the first 20 years of his marriage. But he prays for his wife, Rebekah, and God causes her to conceive twins, Esau and Jacob.

Although **Esau** is tough, he is spiritually dull. **Jacob** is instigating and conniving like his mother. The older twin, Esau, is tricked out of his birthright and blessing respectively by his younger brother and mother.

God chooses Jacob long before He changes his name to . . . **Israel!** Hence, the nation of Israel. Turns out deception runs in Jacob's family. After besting his brother twice, Jacob ends up on the other end of a bait-and-switch. Uncle Laban gives Leah to Jacob as a wife after he works seven years for her sister Rachel. Although Jacob sets out to marry only Rachel, he ends up with Rachel, Leah, and each of their handmaidens. From Jacob and these four women descend the twelve tribes of Israel.

Jacob's most famous son is **Joseph.** Because he is also his father's favorite, his jealous brothers sell him into **Egyptian** slavery. Eventually God raises him up to be the equivalent of vice president of Egypt and reunites him with his family who relocates to **Egypt.**

After Joseph dies, everything is stable until a Pharaoh arises who "doesn't know" Joseph. He decides to enslave Joseph's family, now called the Hebrews, who have grown to great numbers in the land. The Hebrews remain enslaved for **400 years** until the time of **Moses.**

Because the Hebrew population grows so rapidly, Pharaoh orders all male Hebrew babies killed. He fears the slaves will turn against him if a foreign country invades. Moses' mother hides her newborn baby boy in a basket and sets it on the Nile River in an effort to save him. None other than Pharaoh's daughter draws the basket from the water and raises him as her own. As an adult, young Moses intervenes in a fight between an Egyptian and one of his Hebrew brothers, killing the Egyptian. He subsequently flees **Egypt** and becomes a shepherd in the land of Midian for forty years before God calls to him from a **burning bush** and sends him back to Egypt to lead the people out of **bondage**.

Although resistant at first, Moses obeys God and after a series of **ten plagues** and a celebration of the first **Passover** leads the Hebrews on their way to the **Promised Land.** Along the way God parts the Red Sea, feeds His people manna, and leads them with a cloud by day and a pillar of fire at night. Although the people arrive at the Promised Land quickly, ten of twelve spies sent into the land report a population of giants. Instead of trusting God's promise, the people shrink back in fear. God accordingly makes them wander in the wilderness for forty years before they finally enter the Promised Land.

Moses sees the Promised Land from afar but **Joshua** crosses the Jordan and brings the people into it. Under his leadership the famed walls of Jericho fall and the people, more or less, follow God. When

Joshua dies, though, the people return to their wandering ways, lured into sin by the peoples in the land they have not driven out.

Into this rebellious situation, God sends **judges** to deliver the people when they call to Him for help. Some of the more notable judges include **Deborah, Gideon, Samson, and Samuel.**

During the time of Samuel, however, the people of Israel cry out for a king so they will be like the nations surrounding them. Bad move! In asking for a king, God says they are rejecting not Samuel as a judge but God Himself as their King. Israel, up to this point a theocracy, now changes to a monarchy as God gives the people a human king named **Saul.**

While Saul starts out as a hesitant king, even hiding from the masses at the beginning, he becomes quite full of himself before long and falls out of favor with God by his blatant disobedience. Because of his rebellion, God chooses another to be king in Saul's place—not one of his descendants but a shepherd named **David.**

Before David becomes king, we hear of his exploits in killing the giant Goliath, of his deep friendship with Jonathan, King Saul's son, and of his marriage to King Saul's daughter, Michal. Pursued ferociously by King Saul because he is perceived as a threat to his kingdom, David lives on the edge for several years before King Saul finally takes his own life in battle and David ascends to the throne.

Called a "man after God's own heart," David's life exemplifies seeking and following God with the glaring exception of his double sin of adultery and murder. Bathsheba was married to one of David's soldiers, Uriah. One day when David's men are out fighting wars, David sees Bathsheba bathing. Immediately taken by her beauty, David sends for her. One thing quickly leads to another and before long, David creates a soap opera of adultery and murder, killing Uriah after unsuccessfully attempting to cover up Bathsheba's pregnancy.

The prophet Nathan confronts David with his sin and David confesses and takes Bathsheba as another wife. Their baby dies as part of the judgment on David's sin but Bathsheba eventually bears David's son Solomon. Solomon succeeds his father as king but not before David's other sons, notably Absalom, make a run at the throne.

Solomon builds a permanent **temple** for the Lord. David had not been allowed to do this because, although he had followed God with all of his heart, he had been a man of bloodshed and war. Solomon is best remembered for his wealth and wisdom. Ironically, his lack of wisdom with women becomes his undoing. God clearly said foreign wives lead to foreign gods. Solomon disregards these words to his downfall.

Solomon accommodates his many foreign wives' idolatry and eventually it turns his heart away. Because of this, God tears the kingdom from him and from his son **Rehoboam,** who is not a good man. God tears the majority of the kingdom—10 tribes—out of his hand, leaving him only a small part because of His promise to David.

228

This is where it gets a little complicated, but once you grasp this a big part of the Old Testament history will come together for you. Under Saul, David, and Solomon, Israel was one country with one king, a monarchy over twelve tribes. When God tears the kingdom away from Rehoboam, we begin a period called the **divided monarchy.** Rehoboam becomes king of the Southern Kingdom or **Judah** (comprised of the two tribes of Judah and Benjamin) while the Northern Kingdom or **Israel** (comprised of the other ten tribes) is given to Solomon's former servant Jeroboam. The capital of the Southern Kingdom is **Jerusalem**; the capital of the Northern Kingdom is, eventually, **Samaria**. Details? Yes. Important? Extremely!

Until you grasp this history of the division of the kingdom, much Old Testament prophecy and even later historical books will be confusing for you. With reasonable understanding, however, you'll be able to jump in and read anywhere in the Old Testament with some degree of ease. So, because of the importance of this, let's quickly review:

Northern Kingdom
- Israel
- 10 Tribes
- Non-Davidic
- Capital: Samaria

Southern Kingdom
- Judah
- 2 Tribes
- Davidic Line
- Capital: Jerusalem

Once the kingdom divides, a series of kings follows. The kings of Israel are bad, always bad. Okay, Jehu had some good moments, but generally you can remember this: Israel, all bad, all the time.

The kings of Judah, on the other hand, are a mixed bag. Some are horrible, others okay, and at least one you could name a child after. More are bad than good and most of the good ones have reasonable shortcomings. But as a group they prove to be better than Israel, which is why the ax falls on them later than it does on their brothers to the North.

Elijah and **Elisha** prophesy during the time of the divided kingdom. The other prophets are sprinkled throughout the times of the monarchy, the captivity, and the post-captivity.

If you hate historical dates, you may be inclined to skip over the next section. Please don't. Unlike most history that is fraught with countless crucial dates, there are two dates you particularly need to remember in studying the Old Testament. The first is **722 BC**, the second is **586 BC.** Others are important but . . . lose sleep over these two!

By 722 BC the nation of **Assyria** has conquered and deported the Northern Kingdom of Israel as was prophesied. After deporting Israel and dispersing the people, Assyria resettles people from other nations in the land of Israel who have intermarried with remaining Israelites creating a half-breed group called the **Samaritans**. In the New Testament we see "pure-bred" Jews hating these half-breeds. Due to the deportation to and intermixing within the Northern Kingdom, these peoples are often referred to as "the ten lost tribes of Israel."

Seeing their brothers carried away by Assyria does not have the impact on the Southern Kingdom it should. Although it takes a little longer—offset by pockets of revival along the way (notably one under King Josiah)—eventually Judah goes the way of Israel. In 586 BC Jerusalem falls to Babylon, the temple is destroyed, and Nebuchadnezzar (who has already deported people in 605 and 597 BC) continues taking people away into **captivity in Babylon**.

One notable person (a prophet) carried off to Babylon is **Daniel**. To me one of the most prominent vegetable-eaters of all time, Daniel, along with his three friends Shadrach, Meshach, and Abednego, are subjugated in Babylon. The three are thrown into a fiery furnace when they refuse to bow down to a golden statue but the Lord saves them. Daniel likewise is thrown into a den of lions because he continues to pray to his God after prayer to anyone but the king is outlawed. God saves him too.

After seventy years of captivity in Babylon, the people of Judah are released to go back to Jerusalem and rebuild the temple.

Nehemiah is in charge of rebuilding the wrecked walls of the city.

Between the end of the Old Testament and the beginning of the New Testament is a period of **400 years** some refer to as **"The Silent Years."**

Just prior to Jesus' birth God speaks again to His people beginning with His Word to **Zacharias** foretelling of the coming of **John the Baptist** who will prepare the way of the Lord.

231

GO DEEP · GO WIDE · GO TOGETHER

Quick Book Summaries

Whatever you do, don't read these quickie summaries and think you've got yourself a handle on the whole Bible. I have been studying for years, but am still a learner myself. So, from one learner to another, here are some observations on what you'll find in the books of the Bible, and whether the books are easy to read, moderate in difficulty, or just plain difficult according to the subjective Pam-scale. Remember, "difficult" doesn't mean you can't understand them, just that they might not be crystal clear the first (or second) time around, and "easy" doesn't mean that there won't be any sticky issues of interpretation or application!

OLD TESTAMENT

THE BOOKS OF THE LAW

Genesis – Starts with the creation of the earth. Major storyline follows the lives of Adam, Noah, Abraham, Isaac, Jacob, and Joseph. Fifty chapters. Easy reading.

Exodus – Begins in Egypt with a new king (pharaoh) coming to power who did not know Joseph and what he had done for Egypt. Tells of the enslavement of the Israelites and their eventual exodus (leaving) from Egypt by the power of God. The main human character in the book is Moses. In Exodus, we have the giving of the Law at Mt. Sinai and the institution of the tabernacle with a great deal of instructions relating to it, its contents, and the priests. The low point of the book is the making of the golden calf while Moses is receiving the Law from God. Forty chapters. Moderate reading.

Leviticus – Rules and regulations for Israel! What sacrifices were required? What was required of the priest? Of the people? In the book of Leviticus we see what was required of a sinful people in the presence of a holy God. This book is often the undoing of people who try to read through the Bible in a linear fashion. Twenty-seven chapters. Difficult reading.

Numbers –Yes, Numbers has lots of numbers as the people are "numbered" by tribe and more instructions are given on sacrifices and offerings. But for a book that starts off with less than a bang, Numbers boasts some extremely memorable accounts from the wilderness wanderings, including Miriam (the sister of Moses) being struck with leprosy, Israel sending the spies into the Promised Land, and Korah, a rebellious Levite, being swallowed alive by the ground (bet you never heard that story in Sunday School!). Numbers also includes such memorable stories as the bronze serpent in the wilderness and Balaam's donkey. Thirty-six chapters. Moderate reading.

Deuteronomy – Moses' life is drawing to a close and the children of Israel are just about to enter the Promised Land under the leadership of Joshua. With this background, Moses speaks to Israel reminding them of the works of God and calling them to obedience to the covenant and laying out for them the blessings and curses associated with keeping or breaking the covenant. After giving the commands to Israel on the east side of the Jordan River, Moses dies at the end of the book, being remembered in Deuteronomy 34:10b as one whom "the Lord knew face to face." Thirty-four chapters. Moderate reading.

HISTORY

Joshua – One of my favorites! God leads Joshua (Moses' successor) and the people of Israel across the Jordan River and into the land which He had promised to Abraham way back in Genesis. In this historical book, we find the familiar stories of Rahab the harlot and the toppling of the walls of Jericho. We also meet the incredible spy, Caleb, who followed the Lord fully! Throughout the book, we see both the results of obedience and the consequences of sin. Twenty-four chapters. Easy reading (with the exception of a few chapters on the division of the land among the tribes of Israel).

Judges – After the death of Joshua, individual judges raised up by God lead the people of Israel. Judges is a book of cycles. The people forget God and sin against Him. God brings judgment against them in the form of oppression from other nations. When the people wake up and cry out to God for help, God sends a deliverer for them. They typically behave well enough while the judge is alive and then upon the death of the judge fall away and get thumped again. Some of the more memorable judges include Deborah, Gideon, and Samson. Twenty-one chapters. Easy reading.

Ruth – Biography of Ruth, a Moabite woman who becomes part of the line of Christ. Her faithfulness to her Israelite mother-in-law Naomi is legendary. Ruth marries the son of Naomi when Naomi, her husband, and two sons come to live in the land of Moab during a famine in Israel. While in Moab, Naomi's husband dies. Later, when both of her sons die, she decides to return to Israel. Ruth insists on going with her and the rest is history. Four chapters. Easy reading.

I Samuel – The book begins with the life of Samuel, the last judge in Israel, and ends with the life and death of Saul, the first king in Israel. Although mentioned in the lineage in the book of Ruth, David makes his first appearance in I Samuel. He kills Goliath, strikes up a friendship with Jonathan (King Saul's son), and spends much of the book fleeing from King Saul. Thirty-one chapters. Easy reading.

II Samuel – II Samuel follows King David's ascension to power. It includes the account of David and Bathsheba and the death of David's son Absalom. Ending on an uncharacteristic low note in David's life (right down there, so to speak, with the Bathsheba event), the book draws to a close with the wrath of God being poured out against Israel in the form of pestilence in the land for three days as a result of David's sin of taking a census and numbering the people. Twenty-four chapters. Easy reading.

I Kings – Beginning with the death of King David, I Kings follows the kingdom of Israel under David's son King Solomon as he asks wisdom of God and subsequently builds the temple at Jerusalem. In spite of all his wisdom, Solomon allows foreign women and their gods to turn his heart from the Lord. Because of this, God divides the kingdom under Solomon's arrogant son, Rehoboam, leaving David's line to rule the Southern Kingdom of two tribes (Judah and Benjamin) often called *Judah*. The Northern Kingdom comprised of the other ten tribes retains the name *Israel*. The remainder of the book tells of the exploits of the kings of Judah and Israel, as well as accounts of the prophets Elijah and Elisha. The book ends with the account of King Ahaziah in Israel and the content continues right into the beginning of II Kings. Twenty-two chapters. Easy reading.

II Kings – A continuation of I Kings, this book follows the kings and kingdom of Israel up to their defeat and deportation by Assyria in 722 BC, and follows Judah to the time of the Babylonian captivity and the fall of Jerusalem in 586 BC. The taking up of Elijah and the ministry of Elisha are also covered in II Kings. Twenty-five chapters. Easy reading.

I Chronicles – Heavy on the genealogies for the first nine chapters, then moves into chronicling the life of King David for much of the book. Twenty-nine chapters. Difficult reading in chapters 1–9 and 23–27. Easy reading remainder of book.

II Chronicles – Beginning with Solomon and the building of the temple, II Chronicles tells of the subsequent kings of Israel and Judah, following the people of Judah all the way to the time of Cyrus king of Persia who conquered the Babylonian Empire. Thirty-six chapters. Moderate reading.

Ezra – Ezra continues the historical account, picking up the story of the people of Judah in Babylonian captivity and how a group is sent back to Jerusalem by King Cyrus of Persia to rebuild the temple. Ten chapters. Moderate reading.

Nehemiah – The book of Nehemiah tells of the reconstructing of the wall of Jerusalem and the renewing of the covenant after the Babylonian exile. Thirteen chapters. Moderate reading.

Esther – This book recounts the life of Esther, a Jewess who unwittingly becomes Queen of Persia and saves her people from extermination at the hands of the wicked Haman. Ten chapters. Easy reading.

POETRY AND WISDOM LITERATURE

Job – Why do bad things happen to good people? Even people who don't read the Bible know what it means to suffer like Job. This godly man loses everything but remains faithful to God through severe trials and tragedies. In the end, God restores his health and possessions, but it is a long time in coming. Forty-two chapters. Difficult reading.

Psalms – What a book of worship! King David wrote many of the psalms and as you read, you may recognize that many current worship songs are lifted directly from this portion of the Bible. One hundred fifty chapters. Easy reading.

Proverbs – While many of the psalms are attributed to David, his son Solomon wrote much of Proverbs. The Proverbs give practical advice on living, not promises *per se,* but the results that generally follow from a given set of actions. Thirty-one chapters. Easy reading.

Ecclesiastes – Written by Solomon, a man who had everything, Ecclesiastes concludes that all life has to offer apart from God is vanity. Twelve chapters. Moderate reading.

Song of Solomon – A love story written by Solomon. Shows the high biblical view of physical love within marriage. Not a good place to start your children reading the Bible. Eight chapters. Moderate reading.

MAJOR PROPHETS

Isaiah – Writing to the Southern Kingdom of Judah before they are taken into captivity by Babylon, Isaiah warns of coming judgment but also speaks about the future Messiah and the millennial kingdom. Tradition says that Isaiah was eventually martyred by being sawn in two. Sixty-six chapters. Difficult reading.

Jeremiah – Jeremiah also prophesied to Judah, but after the time of Isaiah. Jeremiah is often referred to as the weeping prophet. He continually characterizes Judah as having stiff necks and ears that will not listen. They are stubborn with evil hearts, yet we have in this prophet the view toward the new covenant when God will write His laws on the hearts of His people (Jeremiah 31) and cause them to walk in His ways. Fifty-two chapters. Difficult reading.

Lamentations – Generally attributed to Jeremiah, the book of Lamentations laments the fall of Jerusalem to Babylon. Five chapters. Moderate reading.

Ezekiel – Ezekiel prophesied to the people of Judah who had been taken into captivity in Babylon. He writes of great visions of God, but the end of the book is difficult to wade through in its detailed description of a yet-future temple, probably during the millennial kingdom. Forty-eight chapters. Difficult reading.

Daniel – Taken into captivity in Babylon during his youth, Daniel rose to power under different leaders, but never compromised in his unswerving devotion to his God. The book of Daniel contains some difficult prophetic sections, in addition to the well-known stories of Daniel in the lion's den and Shadrach, Meshach, and Abednego in the fiery furnace. Twelve chapters. Mixture of easy and difficult reading.

MINOR PROPHETS

Hosea – Don't like your job? Just consider the job this guy is given. God tells Hosea to marry a prostitute as a picture of God's faithful love to Israel even though she is continually unfaithful to Him. Hosea prophesied to the Northern Kingdom of Israel. Fourteen chapters. Moderate reading.

Joel – Joel writes to Judah, the Southern Kingdom, prior to the Babylonian captivity and speaks of locusts, destruction, and ultimate deliverance. Three chapters. Moderate reading.

Amos – A shepherd from Judah, Amos was sent to prophesy to the Northern Kingdom of Israel prior to their fall to Assyria. Nine chapters. Moderate reading.

Obadiah – Obadiah prophesies against the descendants of Esau, the people of Edom. One chapter. Moderate reading.

Jonah – Jonah, probably the most famous of the minor prophets, is sent not to the people of Israel or Judah, but to the wicked city of Ninevah. When he decides not to do his job, Jonah is swallowed by a great fish before he finally repents and delivers the message God has for him to give. Four chapters. Easy reading.

Micah – Micah of Moresheth prophesied to Judah well before the Babylonian captivity. He speaks of coming judgment, but also of a coming ruler "From the days of eternity" who will go forth from Bethlehem. Hmm, wonder who that could be? Seven chapters. Moderate reading.

Nahum – Nahum prophesies to Judah, the Southern Kingdom, prior to the Babylonian captivity. His message is the coming judgment against Ninevah, the capital of Samaria, that had conquered the Northern Kingdom of Israel. Three chapters. Moderate reading.

Habakkuk – Habakkuk prophesies to Judah of the impending judgment coming at the hand of Babylon. He questions why God is using evil Babylon to judge His people. Three chapters. Moderate reading.

Zephaniah – Another prophet to Judah, Zephaniah also spoke of the coming judgment by Babylon, yet looks forward to the blessings of the millennial kingdom. Three chapters. Moderate reading.

Haggai – Haggai wrote after the Babylonian exile to call the people to finish the reconstruction of the temple. Two chapters. Moderate reading.

Zechariah – Like Haggai, Zechariah called the people to finish rebuilding the temple. Zechariah is filled with many references to the coming Messiah. Fourteen chapters. Moderate reading.

Malachi – Malachi wrote after the people had returned from captivity to their homeland. Apparently conquest by their enemies was far enough in the past that the people were once again drifting away from God. Four chapters. Moderate reading.

NEW TESTAMENT

THE GOSPELS
Matthew, Mark, and Luke are often termed the synoptic (from a Greek word meaning "same view") Gospels. They each chronicle the life of Jesus Christ but are written to different audiences. In the synoptics, some accounts are recorded by all three evangelists, some by two, others by only one of the three.

Matthew – Matthew wrote to a Jewish audience. The Sermon on the Mount appears in Matthew 5–7. Much of Jesus' teaching in this Gospel has to do with what the kingdom of God is like. It is like a mustard seed, like leaven, like a treasure hidden in a field. Twenty-eight chapters. Easy reading.

Mark – Mark wrote to a Roman audience. He also wrote, by far, the shortest of the Gospel accounts. Sixteen chapters. Easy reading.

Luke – Luke, the physician, wrote to "Theophilus," his Greek, Gentile friend. Luke is also the author of the book of Acts. Luke features the Christmas story that may be read at your house on Christmas Eve—it always is at mine—that is found in Luke 2:1-20. Also notable in Luke is the story of Zaccheus. Twenty-four chapters. Easy reading.

John – John the Apostle takes a different approach in writing his Gospel. He tells us that he has written "that you may believe that Jesus is the Christ, the Son of God; and that believing, you may have life in His name" (John 20:31b). Unlike the synoptic Gospels that take a more chronological approach, John's outline follows seven major signs performed by Jesus. Twenty-wonderful chapters. Easy reading.

THE HISTORY OF THE EARLY CHURCH
Acts – In Acts, Luke, the author of the Gospel bearing his name, recounts the birth of the church. He tells of the ascension of Christ, the

coming of the Holy Spirit, the martyrdom of Stephen, the preaching of Peter, and the conversion and subsequent ministry of Paul. Twenty-eight chapters. Easy reading.

THE EPISTLES (LETTERS)

Romans – In his most thorough discussion of doctrine, Paul explains the righteousness of God in the letter to the Romans. Excellent book to ground new Christians. Sixteen chapters. Moderate reading.

I Corinthians – You think your church has problems? The Corinthians did, too. In this letter, Paul discusses such issues as divisions in the church, problems of gross immorality, marriage and divorce, as well as other topics. Sixteen chapters. Easy reading.

II Corinthians – Really, you have to figure a church with as many problems as Corinth was going to take more than one letter! Thirteen chapters. Easy reading.

Galatians – Confused on the relationship of the Christian to the Law? Galatians is the book for you! Often considered a mini-Romans, Paul emphasizes that the way to God is through faith alone, not working your way to Him. This is the book where you'll find the fruit of the Spirit listed. Six chapters. Easy reading.

Ephesians – Paul writes the church at Ephesus telling them who they are "in Christ," and what this means as they live their lives. Six chapters. Easy reading.

Philippians – In the letter to the Philippians, Paul covers topics including joy, unity, and humility. Four chapters. Easy reading.

Colossians – Need to brush up on the person and work of Jesus Christ? Soak in Colossians for a couple of weeks! Four chapters. Easy reading.

I Thessalonians – Unlike the Corinthian church, the church at Thessalonica was apparently doing the job, and Paul tells them to "excel still more." In addition to other topics, Paul addresses the question of "the day of the Lord." Five chapters. Easy reading.

II Thessalonians – Paul spends much of this epistle setting people straight on the day of the Lord. Three chapters. Moderate reading.

I Timothy – Paul packs a number of contemporary issues into this one as he addresses the topics of church leadership and women in the church. Six chapters. Easy reading.

II Timothy – Just before his martyr's death, Paul writes to his son in the faith, Timothy, to pass the baton and remind him to guard the gospel (1:14) with which he has been entrusted, and to pass it along to faithful men who will be able to teach others also (2:2). Four chapters. Easy reading.

Titus – Paul writes to tell Titus to exhort the church in sound doctrine and to engage in good deeds. He is to appoint elders and instruct those in the church on how to live in a manner that honors Christ. Three chapters. Easy reading.

Philemon – This is a personal letter from Paul to Philemon regarding his runaway slave Onesimus, who had come to faith in Christ. One chapter. Easy reading.

Hebrews – The author of Hebrews exhorts a primarily Jewish church facing persecution to consider Jesus, its merciful and faithful high priest who is able to save forever. Knowing this, they are to hold fast, to draw near, and to press on to maturity. Thirteen chapters. Some difficult subject matter, but wonderful reading.

James – I always get a good "toe-steppin'" from the book of James. Sure, the first thing that many associate with James is the concept of faith and works, but it's always the teaching on the tongue that has me confessing. Five chapters. Easy reading.

I Peter – The apostle Peter speaks on topics including the relationship of the husband and wife, and the issue of suffering in the lives of those who follow Christ. Five chapters. Easy reading.

II Peter – In a letter that has many similarities to Jude's, Peter stresses the concept of true knowledge of God in the face of false teachers. Three chapters. Easy reading.

I John – Wondering if you really have eternal life? Read I John; that's why the apostle John wrote this letter. Five chapters. Easy reading (even in Greek).

II John – In this short letter, John talks about walking in the truth and abiding in the teaching of Christ. One chapter. Easy reading.

III John – This is a personal letter from the apostle John to a man named Gaius dealing with a specific problem in the church. One chapter. Easy reading.

Jude – Jude, the half-brother of Jesus, writes to tell the church to contend earnestly for the faith. He warns of coming judgment citing numerous Old Testament examples yet assures that God is able to keep them from stumbling and to make them stand before His presence blameless with great joy. One chapter. Moderate reading.

PROPHECY

Revelation – The apostle John writes a prophetic book that has yet to see its ultimate fulfillment. Awesome pictures of heaven and exhortations to endure. Do I understand it all? No. Do I love it? Yes. Twenty-two chapters. Difficult reading, but worthwhile if for no other reason (and there are many other reasons) than to see the descriptions of the throne of God and of heaven. Let me whet your appetite:

> ### Revelation 21:22-23
> *And I saw no temple in it, for the Lord God the Almighty and the Lamb are its temple. And the city has no need of the sun or of the moon to shine on it, for the glory of God has illumined it, and its lamp [is] the Lamb.*

Hosting a Bible Reading Retreat

THE VISION

Imagine the people in your sphere of influence falling in love with the Word of God. Imagine yourself falling more in love with God through His Word. Think about the potential for changed lives!

Ignite Bible Reading Retreats foster an environment and create opportunity and space to help people fall in love with the Word of God and the God of the Word by reading the Bible aloud in community.

Learning the Bible is a lifelong undertaking. A weekend in the Word will not substitute for sustained Bible reading and study, but it can serve as a launch catalyst into the Word for some and will cultivate a growing love for the Word in others.

Our hope for Ignite Bible Reading Retreats is that God's people will gain confidence in reading their Bibles, understand God's Word better by reading large chunks with extended context, and ultimately fall more in love with God through His Word.

HOSTING A RETREAT

While hosting a reading retreat is relatively simple, we've outlined some basics to make your retreat even easier to plan!

BEFORE THE RETREAT — LOGISTICS

BUILD A TEAM

Many hands make light work. While this is a simple retreat to host, there are still enough moving parts that you'll be grateful to have help. And, hey, throwing a gathering of any type is always more fun when you can plan with friends!

DETERMINE DETAILS

DATE. Choose a weekend that works best for you, your family (particularly if hosting in your home), and your team.

LOCATION will determine if people spend the night, commute, or a combination of both. If hosting overnight guests, make sure each person has their own bed and that they are informed in advance if they will be sharing a room with others.

COST. Consider food, materials, and lodging (if outside your home).

> **Food** will be your highest cost factor if you host at your church or at home.

> **Lodging** will be the primary cost if you decide on a retreat center or hotel.

> **Materials** are a variable cost. You may decide to purchase Bibles or journals for your group.

You'll set your own price for the weekend to help offset your costs. Unless you are paying for lodging, a registration fee of between $50 and $100 should be enough to cover the cost of meals, snacks, and materials plus leave a little extra should you decide to provide any scholarships.

BEFORE THE RETREAT — CONTENT

Before you start inviting people to your retreat, you'll need to choose your content. Here are some combinations that we've used at past retreats.

KINGS TO JESUS

Your group will binge the life and times of the kings of Israel and Judah and meet the people in the genealogy of King Jesus, as well as dive into Paul's prison epistles and an optional reading of the prophet Jeremiah.

BOOKS YOU'LL READ . . .

- 1 Kings
- 2 Kings
- Matthew
- Galatians
- Ephesians
- Philippians
- Colossians
- Optional: Jeremiah

SUGGESTED RESOURCE

ESV Illuminated Scripture Journal 1 and 2 Kings by Crossway Publishers

ADDITIONAL INFO FOR 1 AND 2 KINGS

Have participants mark references to the Kings of Judah in one color and the Kings of Israel in another color.

BEGINNINGS AND ENDINGS

Your group will read the foundational book of Genesis and the writings of the Apostle John with an optional reading of Isaiah.

BOOKS YOU'LL READ . . .

- Genesis
- John
- 1 John
- 2 John
- 3 John
- Revelation
- Daniel
- Hebrews
- Optional: Isaiah

OLD AND NEW COVENANT

Your group will read through the super-accessible books of Matthew and Proverbs before undertaking one of the most difficult treks in the Bible—Leviticus. Instead of reading straight through, you'll read Leviticus interlaced with the book of Hebrews and see the wonder of Jesus, the once-for-all sacrifice, who fulfills the Law and puts an end to the daily sacrifices that could never take away sin. The retreat will end in Paul's pastoral epistles.

BOOKS YOU'LL READ . . .

- Matthew
- Proverbs
- Leviticus/Hebrews
- 1 Timothy
- 2 Timothy
- Titus

SUGGESTED RESOURCE:
Leviticus/Hebrews interlaced book. Email hello@pamgillaspie.com for additional information.

SELECT, ORDER, PRODUCE MATERIALS

BIBLES
If you have participants whose first language is not English and/or those who struggle with attention deficits, you may want to consider having everyone read from the same translation. You'll often be able to find good pricing for larger quantities at both www.Biblesinbulk.com and www.Christianbook.com.

JOURNALS AND PENS
Journals and pens are a nice touch, but you can also ask people to bring their own.

DURING THE EVENT

MIXING GROUPS
Since reading retreats are a great place to build relationships with one another as well as to deepen our own relationship with the Lord, it can be good to have people read in different groups. This is entirely optional. Here are a few suggestions.

THE DOVE CHOCOLATE METHOD
Have participants draw a Dove chocolate out of a bag to determine their reading group for each session by color. I buy the combo bag with milk chocolate (blue foil), dark chocolate (red foil), and caramel (gold foil).

PLAN A ROTATION
You can plan a rotation to make sure everyone has the opportunity to read with everyone else. This can be helpful if you're team building and want to make sure everyone mixes at some point.

LET THE CHIPS FALL

The wild west approach can also work. Let people make their own choices. If you choose to do this, you'll need to keep an eye open for those who may need a little more help fitting in.

ADDITIONAL INFO

TAKING BREAKS

The only scheduled breaks are typically between sessions, but most groups will want to take an additional break or two so people can use the washroom, stretch, and get snacks. Prompt them to do this at their discretion.

EXTRA SUPPLIES AND NICETIES

You may want to have some of these on hand for day guests:

- Pens, pencils, colored pencils
- A basket of reading glasses
- Extra Bibles—any translation
- Hand sanitizers
- Boxes of Kleenex
- Notecards showing Wi-Fi access info

If you're hosting overnight guests, expect that someone will forget shampoo, conditioner, soap, or tootbrush/paste.

FOOD WRANGLING

READY FOOD ITEMS

If having food catered, call nearby places for prices and ask when you should place your order. Best to have meals delivered or have one person pick up. If preparing food yourself, plan a simple menu.

- Consider what can be made ahead and frozen.
- Consider inviting someone to do this for you.

- Consider asking for attendees' help in preparing the meal.
- Consider requesting that attendees bring ingredients for the meal and having everyone help put it together.

Make plans to accommodate dietary restrictions. Offering gluten-free and vegetarian options that are acceptable to the general population will mean a lot to those attendees who need to restrict certain food groups.

HOW IT LOOKS (sample schedule)

FRIDAY NIGHT

4:00 TO 6:00 P.M. — ARRIVAL AND DINNER

Overnight guests arrive between 4:00 and 6:00 p.m. in order to get settled in rooms.

Commuting guests arrive anytime after 5:00 p.m. with dinner served at 6:00 p.m.

Dinner clean-up by attendees or an assigned person.

You'll begin reading at 7:00 p.m. so consider setting a 6:45 p.m. alarm to remind you to put up food and encourage washroom visits. Final kitchen clean up can be done after 9:30 p.m.

7:00 TO 9:30 P.M. — READING SESSION

Pray as a large group before starting.

Break into groups.

Begin reading at 7:00 p.m.

Take turns reading through the book with each person reading a chapter.

If anyone is uncomfortable with content—for example, a long list of names—they can pass and the next person will pick up.

Take short breaks as needed.

SATURDAY

7:30 TO 8:00 A.M. — CONTINENTAL BREAKFAST

Breakfast should be light and easy like granola, yogurt, smoothies, egg casserole.

If you make this meal heavy, people will not be ready for lunch.

8:00 TO 11:30 A.M. — MORNING READING SESSION

Take turns reading through the book with each person reading a chapter.

Take short breaks as needed.

11:30 TO 12:30 P.M. — LUNCH

Prepare something simple, cater in, or go out.

12:30 TO 2:30 P.M. — AFTERNOON READING SESSION #1 (OPTIONAL)

Note: During the afternoon session, some people need a little more of a break. Let guests know that they can opt out of either the early or later afternoon session if they need a longer break.

2:30 TO 4:00 P.M.— BREAK

People may choose to go for a walk, take a nap, or simply rest and chat.

4:00 TO 6:00 P.M. — AFTERNOON READING SESSION #2 (OPTIONAL)

6:00 TO 7:00 P.M. — DINNER

Prepare something simple, cater in, or go out.

7:00 TO 9:00 P.M. — EVENING READING SESSION

9:00 TO 10:00 P.M. — DEBRIEF AND SHARE

This time will not be content focused. It will focus on the experience of reading extended portions of Scripture in context and vision-casting to encourage people to continue in the Word!

READING RETREAT

FRIDAY

6:00 – 7:00 p.m. Dinner

7:00 – 9:30 p.m. Matthew, part 1

SATURDAY

7:30 – 8:00 a.m. Continental breakfast

8:00 – 11:30 a.m. Matthew, part 2: Proverbs

11:30 – 12:30 p.m. Lunch

12:30 – 2:30 p.m. Leviticus & Hebrews, part 1

4:00 – 6:00 p.m. Leviticus & Hebrews, part 2

[During the afternoon, you can read with the group or choose to spend some quiet time on your own, go for a walk, take a nap ... whatever is restorative to you. Of course, you are always able to opt out of a reading session if you need a break.]

6:00 – 7:00 p.m. Dinner

7:00 – 9:00 p.m. Romans

9:00 – 10:00 p.m. Debrief and Share

SUNDAY

8:00 – 8:30 a.m. Breakfast

8:30 – 9:45 a.m. Selected Psalms

10:00 a.m. On the road to church!

COMBINED

LEVITICUS & HEBREWS

READING

LEVITICUS 1-6

HEBREWS 1-4

LEVITICUS 7-10

HEBREWS 5-7

LEVITICUS 11-17

HEBREWS 8-10

LEVITICUS 18-24

HEBREWS 11-12

LEVITICUS 25-27

HEBREWS 13

FAQs AND COMMON CONCERNS

DOES EVERYONE NEED TO HAVE THE SAME BIBLE?

We encourage people to use their favorite translation (NASB, ESV, KJV, CSB, NET, RSV, NIV, NLT, etc.) and to announce what version they are reading every time they switch groups. Please discourage the use of paraphrases as they are difficult for other readers to follow along and they introduce too much interpretation into the process.

WON'T PEOPLE BE CONFUSED IF WE DON'T STOP TO "STUDY"?

During a reading weekend, participants will read more than they will fully understand, but because of the power of context paired with the speed of intake, most will understand more than they'd ever expect to! Parts of Scripture that are hard to understand when read only a chapter at a time often clear up when a work is read in its entirety in one sitting.

I'M AFRAID I WON'T BE ABLE TO ANSWER THE QUESTIONS THAT MAY COME UP. WHAT DO I DO?!

You keep directing people back to the text. You will be amazed at how many questions answer themselves as you keep reading. You are all learning together, so explain up front that you are not there to be the answer person.

I'M NOT A COOK. DO I HAVE TO PROVIDE FOOD?

No, you can have people arrive after breakfast, do lunch together at a restaurant, then have takeout for dinner.

WHAT IF SOMEONE WANTS TO ATTEND BUT HAS A READING ISSUE?

Invite them to join in by listening!

WILL PEOPLE BE FRUSTRATED IF WE DON'T STOP TO "STUDY"?

With simple "set ups" of content, you'll be providing the basis for further study by reading the full context.

HOW MANY SHOULD I INVITE?

This depends on how much space you have. People are reading out loud, so the sound from one group should not run over into another group in such a way that it creates a distraction or makes it hard to hear. Each reading group should be no larger than 4 to 5 people in order to maintain engagement.

I THINK I CAN HOST A COUPLE OF GROUPS IN MY HOME, BUT I AM CONCERNED THAT THE NOISE FROM ONE GROUP MIGHT SPILL OVER TO THE OTHER GROUP. IS THERE A WAY TO MINIMIZE THAT?

Use some ambient music or nature sounds very low in the background to help block sound carrying from group to group.

Favorite Resources

BIBLE SOFTWARE
Logos Bible Software (Logos.com)
Blueletterbible.com
Biblehub.com

AUDIO BIBLES
The Word of Promise
The Bible Experience

MEMORIZING APPS
Biblememory.com
Bible Memory Tool within Logos Bible Software

SINGLE-VOLUME COMMENTARIES
Moody Bible Commentary
New Bible Commentary

SOME MULTI-VOLUME COMMENTARY SETS THAT I USE REGULARLY
NIV Application Commentary Series
New American Commentary Series
United Bible Societies Handbook Series for Bible Translators

WORD STUDY RESOURCES
A Greek-English Lexicon of the New Testament and Other Early Christian
Literature (aka Bauer)
Theological Dictionary of the New Testament, Abridged (aka Little Kittel)
Enhanced Strong's Lexicon (aka Strong)

STUDY BIBLE
New Inductive Study Bible, Harvest House Publishers

We'd Love to Hear From You!

If you found this study helpful please take
a moment to share your thoughts.

Leave a Review

https://www.pamgillaspieshop.com/products/go-sustainable-strategies-for-engaging-gods-word

OR

Take a Short Survey

https://bit.ly/GObooksurvey